ROBIN HOOD

According to
SPIKE MILLIGAN

ROBIN HOOD

According to
SPIKE MILLIGAN

TED SMART

This edition produced for
The Book People Ltd
Hall Wood Avenue, Haydock
St. Helens WA11 9UL

First published in 1998 by Virgin Publishing Ltd

Reprinted 2000, 2003, 2007

A catalogue record for this book is available from the British Library.

ISBN 978 0 7535 0942 5

Typeset by TW Typesetting, Plymouth, Devon.

Printed and bound in Great Britain by
Mackays of Chatham, Lordswood, Chatham, Kent.

The Legend of Robin Hood

Once upon a time, sometimes twice upon a time, there lived a Lord and Lady Huntingdon. He was seven feet ten inches and she was five feet so they never had to talk when making love. Tiptree was his favourite jam. Tiptree Strawberry Jam: it's delicious when spread on bread and when the jars are empty you can keep water in them. Tiptree is the jam for you.

One day Lady Huntingdon gave birth to a boy. They fed him on steroids. He soon grew to seven feet. The boy was destined to become an outlaw.

'Come one, come all and join me as archers in Sherwood Forest. When we are hungry we'll have jam sandwiches and deer. I, Robin Hood, will lead you with my wonder weapon, a bow and arrow. This puts paid to sword and axe.'

A Norman archer killed King Harold. Robin found the Norman Army, the dead and dying. Many were eating jam sandwiches.

Robin started robbing. He did the Midland Bank, Lloyds and Barbara Streisand. He had her nose fixed.

Robin Hood had a pet duck. He rented it out for children's parties.

The Sad End Of Much The Miller

1

> *The good spirit of Sherwood, 12%,*
> *Sherwood in the twilight,*
> *Is Robin awake?*
> *Grey and ghostly shadows are*
> *Gliding through the break.*
> *Shadows of the dapple deer*
> *Dreaming of the morn,*
> *Dreaming of shadowy men in the winds*
> *Of a shadowy horn,*
> *Aren't you bloody glad you're not bloody well born.*
>
> Alfred Noyes, 'Sherwood', 1903

King Richard the First, Richard Coeur de Lion, came to the throne in 1189 and left it a year later leaving a debt of £500,000. All lost on the bingo table. He set off to free Jerusalem from the Saracens and bingo. He used to ride past them and set fire to their legs. John, his brother, was a truly merciless man. He wore no trousers. John rode with his bandits to the Sheriff of Nottingham's second-hand-car and scrap-yard business, where he shared some of the profits.

They had reached a lightly wooded area of the great Sherwood Forest when suddenly a man started to shout. 'Save me, Prince. In God's love, save me!'

'Who is he?' asked John casually.

'They call him Much. He was a miller once but he was much too fond of the King's deer,' his Lieutenant replied.

'Oh,' said Prince John. 'Why the King's deer? Was there no other way?'

'He couldn't afford to go on eating at McDonald's. He has fallen in with a band of outlaws led by Robin Hood.'

'Describe this Robin Hood.'

'I don't know much of him, sir. Robin Hood comes out of the forest but then goes back in again.'

'Faugh, faugh!' cried Prince John impatiently, which was, in fact, 'fuck' in old English.

So they dragged poor Much away. Suddenly, with a desperate cry, he tore himself loose, snatched a sword from one of the men and made a rush at the Prince's horse's bum, which he stabbed, the horse then throwing the Prince over his head. Alas, the men held Much down; some held him up; some held him sideways. His future looked grim . . . and short. Ahead of him lay only death, torture, excruciating pain and abominable barbarity – but mainly death.

There was a whooshing sound and an arrow sped to Much's heart and laid him dead on the ground. The feather on the arrow was red – the signature of Robin Hood.

'Who loosed that arrow?' cried Prince John.

He turned as he spoke and saw at the edge of the

glade a man wearing a green cloak over his suit of brown and widdling against a tree.

'Who goes there?' called Prince John, pointing to the tree.

'We all do.'

'Tell me, is this Robin Hood, this fellow – is he rich? Are his lands wide?'

'Once they were indeed wide,' said the Lieutenant, 'but now only the house and the lands of Locksley remain to him. The other lands he has sold. He put them on the market with Harrods.'

'Ah, then his coffers would be full of gold,' said John.

'And Harrods' as well,' said the man, 'and Ali Khan's, the owner. I know that this Robert, Earl of Locksley, known as Robin Hood, has some secret need for money. He has an offshore bank account with Lloyds of London in Jersey in the name of Charlie Chaplin and Sons.'

'I didn't know he was a son of Charlie Chaplin.'

'That may well be, but he remains a dangerous enemy,' said the Lieutenant.

'How may we put an end to his treachery?' asked the Prince.

'Then I'll tell thee how it can be done. Tomorrow the Loony Earl of Locksley is to be married at Fountains Abbey.'

'Then there we will deal with the cursed Robin Hood,' cried the Prince.

They rode off into the grey of the evening, leaving the body of old Much le Miller lying where it had fallen. His wife had already collected the insurance policy and was living at the Ritz.

*

As his men gathered in the clearing, Robin Hood mused over the death of Much. It had been the merciful thing to do. No one stabbed the Prince's horse up the bum and got away with it.

When the King Richard came back from the crusade, things would be better. For a start he'd have Much buried! But if he never came back that devil Prince John would be King and God have mercy on everyone.

A man walked into the midst of the occasion.

'Will Scarlet,' called out Robin Hood, 'my true friend. What have you got there?'

'I have brought a hundred sausages for the feast and a hundredweight of chip potatoes from Marks & Spencer's.'

'God's blessing on you, Robin Hood,' they all chorused, except the boy who was kneeling by his father's body. He wept copiously on the corpse. If Much had been alive, he'd have drowned.

'So they have killed old Much. Have comfort, boy, be at peace,' said Robin. 'He has been spared many evils – income tax, overdraft, mortgages, bills and AIDS.'

'Let me come with you, Robin, and serve with you,' pleaded the boy. 'Look, I'm old enough: I have hairs on my willy.'

'Oh, well done, son, and I might say well hung.'

How Robert Of
Locksley Became
An Outlaw

2

In Locksley Hall that night all seemed peaceful after the gigantic meal. There was burping, leaping, being sick and farting. They all feasted in honour of Robert Fitzooth Locksley's wedding to Marian Fitzwalter, which was to take place on the morrow as soon as they'd washed all the vanilla and chocolate ice cream off the bridal gown.

Earl Robert stood near the great fireplace, welcoming his guests and collecting five dollars a head – the mean bastard!

Lady Marian Fitzwalter stood beside him. She was some five years younger than he was. She was tall and beautiful and had won the hundred-metre gold medal. She could also pole vault anything up to twenty feet. She had practised over Earl Robert two or three times during the evening. She could also hop, skip and jump twenty feet.

They now drank a toast to the bride and groom. They held up their drinking horns, which were edged with gold. 'Here's to Robin and Marian,' they said. They drank the toast; it was water. One of the hidden traits of Robin was meanness.

Finally the drunken guests sang the following boring chant: 'Pray Ye Do It For Prosperity'.

Boring Chant

Down with John.
Drink to the Lion Hearted
Everyone.
Especially long live Richard
Robin and Richard.
Down with John.
Drink to the Lion Hearted
Everyone.
God bless
Ronny Scott.

'Hello, what have we here?' said someone.

Well, someone had spotted something that was here, but he never said what it was.

As the boring song ended there was a groan of relief. A portly monk, dressed in russet robes, appeared with a haircut that made him look like he had a lump on his head. He also got a groan of relief as he pushed his way through the throng. Suddenly, and for no reason at all, he fell backward like a board. He'd found the drink.

In the luxurious surroundings of the Sheriff of Nottingham's second-hand car lot, Prince John brooded over his forthcoming encounter with Robin Hood.

'Your Highness, when I enquired from Much the Miller's son, who has hairs on his willy, he told me all was well with him and Scarlet had come to take him away to be cared for by Robin Hood,' the Sheriff said.

'Will Scarlet, Robin Hood . . .' roared Prince John, clutching his crown and knocking it off to the floor with a loud clang.

From under the banquet table came drunken voices: 'Long live Richard, Robin and Richard.' And there it stopped. They had fallen asleep.

'Yes, there is no doubt about it,' continued Prince John. 'Tomorrow, curtail the wedding of this traitor, Robin, or Robin Declared An Outlaw, and you take and hang him forthwith. There, of course, are his lands and his goods, which are forfeit to me. And that attractive bride of his, Lady Marian. Trouble is, as soon as I get near her − she is a champion − she pole vaults twenty feet over me. I try to catch her; she does one hundred metres in twelve seconds. If I try to trap her she does the hop, skip and jump, twelve, ten, twenty feet.'

Lord Fitzwalter, Lady Marian's father, seemed troubled and uneasy. He suffered with piles and acne.

Yes, this was the day of the wedding of Robin to Marian. They stood at the altar; it seemed a good place for it.

'Hold,' said a Knight, arriving with a detail of armed guards. 'I am Guy de Custard Gisborne, come in the King's name without trousers to stop this ceremony proceeding. Pursuivant, read the mandate.'

'Look, will you piss off,' said Robin Hood.

A man dressed in the livery of Sarah Bernhard unrolled the parchment and read in a louce voice. 'Be it all known that Robert Fffffittzzooth, known as Old Mother Riley, and Marian −'

'Let me see that seal,' said Robin. 'It's not genuine.'

Quickly he raised his hunting horn and blew his horn through the window. In no time at all the church was surrounded by Robin's bowmen. In one charge Robin and his men dispersed the Sheriff's men, and then made good their escape into the forest.

'It's no good following him now, but he'll find the Sheriff waiting for him at Locksley Hall if he ventures there,' snorted Sir Guy, cowering by the altar.

But, alas, Robin had ventured somewhere else.

'Robin is one of the finest marksmen with an arrow. He can shoot through the seams of a man's trousers and out the other side. It's a dangerous thing to outlaw such a man,' boomed the Priest, Brother Michael. 'You have taken his home. Where will he live?'

'He might have to go into B&B.'

'You have taken his cattle. What will he eat?'

'Well, there's Big Macs, Kentucky Fried Chicken, takeaway vindaloo curry.'

'I am Lady Marian's confessor,' said Brother Michael. 'She has beauty, grace and £100,000 in the Bank of Australia.'

The Outlaws Of Sherwood Forest

3

A hundred valiant men has this brave Robin Hood
Still ready at his call those bowmen were right good
All clad in Lincoln green with caps of red and blue
His fellows winded horns not one of them new
All made of Spanish yew, his bows were wondrous strong
They did not an arrow draw but was a cloth yard long
They drew a wondrous arrow that could get through gaps
That rarely missed their mark
They really missed when they missed Hyde Park.

Early next morning Sir Guy de Custard Fitz Gisborne set out for Arlington, home of the Fitzwalters. His guide was the Fat Friar called Brother Michael who so disgraced himself on the eve of the wedding of Robin Hood. The Abbot had banished him in no uncertain terms.

'You go out, false and treacherous man, as you came in many years ago, plain Michael Tuck, no longer a brother of this order. If you show your face around here again, I'll shut the door in your face,' the Abbot had cried.

15

'I haven't got a door in my face. Why then,' cried the Friar gaily, 'farewell to the Abbey of Fountains, and all hail to the jolly green coat and catch me again if you can.'

So he went on his way singing: 'We'll meet again, Don't know where, Don't know when . . .'

As they came in sight of Arlington Castle, the Friar ceased from his singing in case they thought he was being tortured.

'You best turn back, Sir Knight, or at the least lower that visor of yours,' he advised Sir Guy.

'How?' exclaimed Guy Sir Gisborne. 'Surely Lord Fitzwalter is not in league with Robin Hood.'

'Far from it,' laughed the Fat Friar. 'Lady Marian Fitzwalter assuredly is, and she is national pole vault champion at eighteen and stays at the YWCA.'

They reached the castle in safety, however, and Lord Fitzwalter welcomed them loudly, showing great eagerness to be on the side in power, and the YWCA!

Lord Fitzwalter was deep in discussion with his aspirant son-in-law, Robin Hood.

'Would you have had me marry my daughter to an outlaw, a fly-by-night, a slayer of deer, an Old Mother Riley impressionist?'

'For her I save my nether regions,' said Robin.

'Just wait till I get a chance to get to your nether regions,' said Lord Fitzwalter. 'You will never see them again. The marriage was never completed!'

'Will you stop saying that or I will crush your balls between my teeth,' said Robin.

Lord Fitzwalter was going more and more red in fury for at this moment Lady Marian came suddenly into the room, clad in topless green with a quiver of arrows at her side and a bow in her hand.

'What now? Where are you off to now, wench?'

'The *Sun*. I'm a page-three girl,' Marian calmly answered.

'That you shall not,' bellowed Fitzwalter. 'I will have up the drawbridge.'

'I shall pole vault it,' said Marian.

'But I will secure the gates.'

'But I will pole vault anything up to twenty feet.'

'I will lock you in your upper chamber three hundred feet up.'

And suddenly she exclaimed, 'Father, let me go to the greenwood. You have my promise that I will return and I promise that Robin will do nothing to me more than he is doing now without your leave.'

'All right, just this once,' said Lord Fitzwalter.

'And now,' said Robin, 'those who remain with me, let us go away to our new home in the forest where it's pouring bloody rain and see how many of us are still alive after the attendant illnesses we'll gather. We stand loyally together for the King; for God; for his anointed servant Richard, King by the Divine Right; and for justice and the righting of wrongs and pneumonia.'

And they all got pneumonia. Robin went on boring the men with his speech for another half an hour by which time they had all contracted pneumonia. Some of them tried to get out of the contract but they hadn't read the small print.

So they went to the forest of greenwood, with steep banks fencing in either side and in which there were caves both deep and dry at either end of a shallow valley out of which floods of water were issuing. The forest edged them in with mighty trees of oak and ash and beech, frogs and leeches, and thick clumps of impossible thorn with desolate marshes where a horse might disappear for ever. It was run with ferocious rivers. Robin went along the footway and fell into a deep river.

'Help! Help!' he said. 'I can't swim! I can't swim!'

And Friar Tuck was walking by and said, 'Look, I can't play the violin but I don't go shouting it around to everybody.'

That night Robin hosted a great feast of venison. Many of the vegetarians settled for veggie burgers.

He decided to go for a wander through the secret lanes of Sherwood Forest. He had to stop twenty times to find the way. Finally he mounted his horse and galloped over the bridge and straight into the lake.

'Help! Help! I've fallen in the water! Help! I can't swim!'

A man passing by said, 'Here, catch this,' and threw him a ship.

Finally the archers sent a search party out for him and they spent half the bloody night looking for him. Eventually they rescued him. After a few brief words they set about lighting two great fires to roast the venison and in twenty minutes they had half of Sherwood Forest in flames.

Then Robin Hood arose and addressed them. The trouble was they'd heard it all before. He began by telling the men, 'Remember that we are outlaws, not robbers. We must take the King's deer. I mean, we can't live on Big Macs, but when the King returns I myself will beg pardon at his feet for this trespass, and now –' ('Oh dear,' groaned the archers) '– you shall all swear the oath that I must swear with you – Long live King Richard. Kellogg's Corn Flakes are the ideal breakfast food.'

END OF COMMERCIAL

'Thank Christ,' said one of the archers, 'I thought he was going on all bloody night.'

The Rescue Of Will Scarlet

4

And these will strike for England
And man and maid be free
The foil and spoil, the tyrants beneath
The greenwood tree

Tennyson, 'The Foresters', 1881

Early the next morning Robin gathered his band in Sherwood Forest and swore his great oath ('Go and get me some money!').

Walking briskly through the forest and frequently getting lost, Scarlet and Little Much came to the edge of open parkland in the middle of which stood a great stone house set in a lake. Unfortunately, once again Robin's unreliable horse had pitched him into the lake.

'Help! I can't swim!'

The guard on duty said, 'Hang on to the horse.'

'He can't swim either,' said Robin.

And so Robin took drowning lessons.

He dragged himself ashore just as Scarlet and Little Much reached the edge of the lake.

'Have you got me any money yet?' asked Robin, wringing out his tights.

'Alas, no,' replied Scarlet. 'Please accept this humble cheese sandwich as an apology, my Lord Robin.'

'Well, there's a pile of treasure hidden in a secret place in that house,' said Robin. 'All you have to do is cross the lake, evade the guards, find the secret place, steal the gold and jewels, sneak out without being spotted, cross the lake again and get the loot back to me. It's a cinch. I've already drunk half the lake to make it easier for you.'

Scarlet and Little Much left Robin tucking into his sandwich and drying out while they set off to raid the castle. All went according to plan until they came to make their escape with the bounty. As they made their way down a darkened stone staircase, a figure stepped from the shadows. It was Sir Guy de Custard Gisborne.

'Aha,' said Sir Guy. 'What have we here?'

'We have me here,' said Scarlet.

'Stop that man!' cried Sir Guy, drawing his sword. It was a very good likeness.

Scarlet flung open the bundle he was carrying and snatched out the bag of gold and jewels. 'Much,' he hissed, 'guard that with your life.'

'Christ, I might not live that long,' said Little Much.

By now a guard had appeared and grabbed Scarlet. 'What have you got there?'

'I've got me,' said Scarlet.

'What has the knave under his cloak?' roared Sir Guy.

'More of me,' said Scarlet.

But Sir Guy had seen Scarlet's face.

'It's Will Shitlock! Hold him! He's a traitor!'

Scarlet's hand flew to the long knife at his belt but, as he drew it, his trousers fell down. Little Much was long gone and so missed out on the chance to compare willy hair.

'I am no traitor,' said Will Scarlet. 'You be aware of the vengeance of Robin Hood and Co. My card, W Scarlet, Director.'

After this Scarlet was led away into the Great Hall. There was some semblance of a trial before the Sheriff, then, heavily guarded, he was taken to Nottingham and chained in a dungeon.

Much the Miller's son missed his way several times as he trod the narrow path in the heart of the forest. He fell in the bog and came up covered in it. Finally he found himself in the glade and told the news to Robin Hood, after handing him the bag of gold and jewels for which Scarlet had risked his life.

When Robin had heard all that had happened, he was sorely grieved, bringing his fist down into a plate of porridge.

'I'm willing to hang Guy de Custard,' said Robin savagely, banging his fist into a plate of porridge. He was covered in it.

So they marched to attack.

At the edge of the forest Robin fell in a bog. They finally got him out. He was pitch black.

Outside the prison, Robin approached a man he knew to be trustworthy.

'Now tell me, good Palmer,' said Robin Hood, 'do you know Will Shitlock or Scarlet?'

'That I do. I knew him when he was only shit. They brought him in last night. You're pitch black.'

'Never mind all that crap. When do they hang him?'

'He hangs tomorrow at midday before the Sheriff and Prince John,' answered the Palmer.

'They're hanging the Sheriff and Prince John?'

'No, they'll just be there.'

At noon the next day a crowd had gathered around the gallows. Foremost in the crowd was an old beggar leaning on a staff.

'Ere,' said a man with no balls. 'If only Robin Hood were here to give a lead.'

The Sheriff and Prince John sat on a lofty podium to view the execution. To create a diversion, Robin had secreted a haddock in the crotch of Prince John's tights.

Then Scarlet spoke from the gallows. 'My name is Shitlock, also known as Scarlet, and my Robin will save me. I am no grasping villain!'

'Rest assured we shall seek him out,' growled the Sheriff, who was red with anger, white with rage and purple with fury.

At that moment, Prince John collapsed on the podium, overcome with haddock fumes, and the old beggar threw off his ragged cloak. It was Robin! He waved his staff as a signal and in an instant a hundred archers rushed the gallows and carried it off into the forest. Scarlet was saved.

And the crowd sang: 'We'll meet again . . .'

In fact, they met them all again coming out of McDonald's. Each of a hundred archers shot an arrow into a hundred Big Macs as a warning . . .

How Little John Came To The Greenwood

5

You gentlemen and yeomen good
Come in and drink with Robin Hood
If Robin Hood be not at home
Come in and drink with Little John.

Anon, 'William MacGonigal', 1887

After Robin Hood had rescued William Shitlock he remained quietly in Sherwood holding up a baggage train, clubbing innocent travellers insensible and removing all their goods for confiscation. So life settled down at Sherwood Forest. It was so up to date Sherwood Forest was fitted with a burglar alarm. Unfortunately, it caught him six times.

Prince John sent a large force to drive Robin out of Sherwood and they were shot to pieces. The pieces were given back to their widows as souvenirs. Prince John roamed Sherwood, gradually going mad looking for him and foaming at the mouth. Someone tried to shoot him for having rabies and he had to wear a muzzle.

With the supermarkets opening, Robin bought four hundredweight of chip potatoes at Marks & Spencer's.

He would order a dozen Mars bars for distribution for heroism among his archers. But still Robin grew restless.

'Stay you all here, my merry fellows. Come swiftly if you hear the blast of my horn. It means I am in the shit.'

First Ducking Sequence

About noon Robin came across a forest path with a wide, swift-flowing stream cutting across it. (Please God, he's not going to drown again.) On the other side of the stream was a tall yeoman. The stranger carried a long, stout staff, as did Robin.

They faced each other at either side of a log which bridged the stream, but it was wide enough only for one.

'Out of my way, little man,' shouted the stranger, who was a good foot taller than Robin.

'Not so fast, tall fellow,' said Robin, 'and not so tall, fast fellow. Go back until I have passed.'

'Why then, I'll break your head first and dip you into the water afterwards,' cried the stranger.

'We'll see about that. I'm not frightened of water. I can swim,' Robin lied.

'You talk like a bloody fool,' exclaimed the stranger.

Bringing this story to a conclusion, the bloody fool whacked the stranger, who immediately retaliated, sending Robin straight into the water. Robin Hood swam gracefully to the surface, arse first.

Robin dutifully invited the newcomer back to Sherwood Forest and he joined the archers. Little John was his name but he was known as Big Dick because . . .

How Sir Richard Of Legh Paid The Abbot

6

My londes beth set to weddie Robin
Untyll a certayne daye to a rich abbot here besyde of
Saynt mac abbay [Gobble-de-gook]

Anon, 'A Lytelt Geste of
Robyn Hode', 1489

One day soon after he came to the greenwood, Big Dick
was wandering with Robin Hood deep in the wilds of
Barnsdale, the arsehole of England. With them were
Scarlet and Little Much, forming a small party about the
size of the Liberals. They were in search of a hidden site
to make a camp where a whole band could hide if
Sherwood Forest was hit by an atomic bomb while they
waited for it to explode.

'Good master, let us shoot a fat deer for our lunch.
We shall all be the better for a feast.'

'I have no desire to dine yet,' said Robin. 'Give
everyone a jam sandwich and a plate of soup to entice
them. Wait there in hiding until some uninvited guest
asks his way and then bring him to dinner whether he
will or not.'

'What kind of guest would you have?' asked Big Dick.
'A starving one.'

They came back with a noble Knight in rags. He'd been repairing his horse and got covered in oil and shit.

'What master is yours?' asked the Knight.

'Robin Hood,' answered Big Dick.

'Oh, I didn't know he was into haute cuisine.'

'Well, I thank you,' said the Knight when the meal was ended. 'I have not dined so well these past three weeks, during which I lost three stone.'

'Now I must ask you to pay something towards what you have eaten,' said Robin.

'Alas,' said the guest, sighing even more deeply, 'my coffers are empty. There is naught that I can proffer without shame.'

'This Knight is a true Knight, a glutton and skint,' Robin declared. 'Fill him now with a cup of wine. My good mate, did you lose money in usury or women?'

'I played bingo with housekeeping money.'

'How much do you owe on your home?'

'Just four hundred pounds. I owe this sum to the Abbot. If I do not pay it tomorrow, then I'll lose everything – the wife, the horse, the mangle.'

'Big Dick, see if we have four hundred pounds in the treasury.'

'Unfortunately, Robin, all we have in the treasury is two shillings and sixpence,' said Big Dick.

'Well, for all it's worth, you can borrow it and let us have it when you have enough.'

*

Next day.

'God's blessings, my Abbot,' said the Knight. 'I am here within the hour.'

'Have you brought the money you owe me?'

'Come off it,' said the Knight. 'I have two and sixpence as a first instalment.'

'That's no bloody good,' said the Abbot. 'You get no further help from me, Knight that would cheat the Holy Church of four hundred pounds and try to pay it with two and sixpence.'

Sir Richard rode full speed to Legh Hall where his horse collided with his wife.

'My merry good lady, all is well. I have paid the National Debt; our lands are safe for ever. I gave him a two and sixpence postdated cheque as a first instalment.'

At the local bingo hall Robin was losing £3. His men had to drag him away screaming, 'All the fours Dr's orders, legs eleven . . .' Finally he fell asleep on a horse. When he awoke he was twenty miles away.

Maid Marian
Of Sherwood
Forest

7

Gamwell Hall, seat of Robin's uncle, Sir William Custard Gamwell, was not far from Nottingham. And thither Sir Guy Custard de Custard Gisborne rode one day, along with the Sheriff and a body of men.

'Sir Guy, Sheriff, welcome,' said Custard Gamwell, with two Kentucky Fried Chicken and chips, £2.50.

Sir Guy suggested that they all attend the great festival held not far from the forest, hoping (aha!) to find out where Robin Hood was.

Sir Guy de Custard sat quietly under a tree while Sir William was eating a couple of Big Macs. Only once did he lean forward suddenly with an angry glint in his eyes and put on his glasses. An archer led one of the maidens out to dance who will be recognised as Lady Marian Fitzwalter disguised as a *Sun* page-three peasant girl.

'What maiden is that who's dancing with that crippled dancer?' asked Sir Guy.

'Oh, he's a well-known crippled dancer,' said Sir Custard William vaguely. 'She is known as the stupendous Clarinda. She oughtn't to come to these feasts.'

'What is your archer's name?' he asked.

'Robin, I believe,' said Sir William.

'Is that all you know of him?'

'He is inside leg 33 inches, blood group Rhesus negative, inside hat 6⅞.'

'Why, let me tell you,' said Sir Guy sternly. 'He is none other than the outlaw Robert Fitzooth Locksley. Tell me, what would you then advise me to do?'

'Why,' answered Gamwell, 'I would advise you to turn and ride like fuck for Nottingham unless you want a volley of arrows.'

By the time Sir Guy looked round again, Robin and Marian had made good their escape into the forest. Waiting not a moment, Sir Guy assembled his troops and he and the Sheriff set off at a pace, pursuing the renegades into the greenwood.

Waiting in the shelter of the trees, a portly Monk observed the commotion approaching down the forest path.

'Now who be these coming so fast this way?' he pondered. 'The stupendous Clarinda and Robin, I'll be bound, and with Sir Guy de Custard Gisborne in their wake.'

Robin and Marian went right and left into the cover of the trees. He went right and left and then she went right and left. Friar Tuck was left to face their pursuers.

'Out of the way, renegade Friar,' shouted Sir Guy. 'You keep doubtful and traitorous company and you . . .'

At this a hundred arrows rained down on them, decimating the troops and wounding Sir Guy.

The stupendous Clarinda appeared at the side of the path.

40

'As for doubtful and traitorous company, I see none on this side of the forest,' she said, as she pole vaulted the path.

Sir Guy raised his hand derisively as he started to speak and, swift as thought, the stupendous Clarinda raised her bow: the string hummed and Sir Guy's hand was transfixed by an arrow.

'Treachery! Cut them down . . . and sideways!' shouted the Sheriff.

The bow strings hummed again. The Sheriff's horse reared up as an arrow whizzed into the ground between his forefeet and the Sheriff was thrown off backward into a pool of mud.

'Faugh, oh faugh,' he said, 'oh faugh.'

Thereupon, arrows sped among the Sheriff's men, who retreated up a steep embankment only to be beaten back by the mighty staff in the hands of the great Friar. Roaring lustily, he stood there alone whirling his staff from side to side among the Sheriff's men, knocking down one, breaking the ribs of another, flattening the nose of another, cracking the skull of another. Thank heavens they were all in BUPA.

Next morning Lord Fitzwalter was disturbed. A large body of armed men drew up on the further side of the moat, with the Herald blowing his trumpet and an Officer bidding them, 'Lower the drawbridge in the King's name.'

'Ye bugger off-ee,' roared Lord Fitzwalter angrily. 'All balls and hang me arse,' he spluttered without his teeth. 'What do you mean by coming here with this nonsensing story about my daughter, the Lady Marian, bruising the

Sheriff, injuring his men and shooting arrows into Sir Guy de Custard Gisborne? She would never kill a man without knickers. Off you go or I'll bid my men to shoot at you with their crossbows.'

'You'll hear more of this,' shouted the Officer.

'No I won't. I've heard enough already.'

'Not so lightly may you flout the will of our Liege, Lord Prince John.'

'Faugh! Him!' shouted Lord Fitzwalter. 'Let him come in person.'

The troops around the moat could see that an archer with a crossbow stood ready at every loophole, that the drawbridge was up and the moat wide and deep, and boiling oil in a giant pot was being poured over the troops below. It was olive oil at five shillings a bottle. It's lovely with salads.

'And what's this story about the stupendous Clarinda posing topless for the *Sun* on page three? You go no more forth from the castle,' declared Lord Fitzwalter to Lady Marian.

'Then I'll get out if I can,' answered Marian. 'I'll pole vault the moat. Prince John will get me out.'

'You can't bloody tolerate him.'

'Listen! If you shut me up I shall escape from the castle. No blame can be attached to you and you can welcome Prince John here with every sign of regret at my absence and fury at my flight.'

'Hum-ha,' said Lord Fitzwalter, and opened his toothless mouth and popped in a Polo. 'God bless you, Marian, and your pole vault!'

*

A few hours later Prince John rode up with high blood pressure, 180 over 90. Lord Fitzwalter met him at the gate with a most profuse expression of loyalty, begging pardon for his behaviour to the Herald in the morning.

Prince John was graciously pleased to accept Lord Fitzwalter's apologies, grovelling at the same time. When he asked to be presented to the Lady Marian, it was found she was no longer three hundred feet up planning a route for her escape.

Lord Fitzwalter raged around the castle. He raged around it 28 times and got very giddy, his blood pressure 200 over 160. He was dead but he didn't know it.

Prince John graciously lent half his followers to Lord Fitzwalter and they scoured the neighbourhood until it was spotless, but Lady Marian Fitzwalter had vanished.

Another
Confrontation
With Robin

8

Robin came across a young man dressed in forest attire eating a jam sandwich at speed.

'Ah now, good fellow,' cried Robin, 'why so fast?'

'It might escape.'

'Look, I'll wait till you finish your jam sandwich and I'll challenge you to a joust with sticks. Where do you get all this jam from?'

'Lugworth's Jam Factory,' said the youth.

'Does your father own the jam factory?'

'Yes.'

All the while the lad was beating back Robin Hood, who had to say, 'Don't hurt me! Will you stop fighting? I cannot match you. Do you have any more jam sandwiches? I'd like one.'

'I'll get them to post you one.'

Suddenly the young lad took off his beard. 'Robin, don't you know me?'

'Marian,' said Robin, his arms around her squeezing her boobs.

'You've never done that before, Robin.'

'Well, I'm coming of age.'

There was feasting and boob squeezing that night as Robin and his merry men did honour to their queen.

Robin got more and more imbibed. He rose with a flagon in each hand, swaying and spilling it all over him. He fell down, rose again, fell down, stayed down.

Before he started again, his archers fled to bed.

How Sir
Richard Paid
Robin Hood

9

Get well your abbot, sayd Robyn
And your pryour, I you pray,
And byd hym send me such a monke
To dyner every day.

Anon, 'A Lyell'

Sir Richard and his followers hastened along into Barnsdale. They came to a bridge where many people living nearby were meeting that day for a wrestling match. The prize was a white horse with a harness, a pair of gloves, a gold ring, a pipe of wine and a jam sandwich. And, just as Sir Richard arrived, wrestling was taking place. One of the wrestlers had gone home, leaving his opponent on his own to try to win alone. Nobody would take his opponent's place.

'Is this not a contest open to all comers?' asked Sir Richard.

'But the men of Barnsdale be jealous of an outsider like this Arthur A Bland and they fear he will beat our man and throw him in the river,' explained a yokel.

'This shame should not be,' exclaimed Sir Richard.

He pushed his way through the crowd and struck down the cudgels which were raised to fell Arthur A Bland. Sir Richard spoke to the gathering. He appealed to the pride of every Barnsdale man and many came forward to challenge Arthur A Bland. Bland beat the crap out of the lot of them. The white-horse prize then threw him and kicked him in the balls and galloped away.

While Sir Richard was boldly proving yet again what a prat he was, Robin and his men waited in vain for him to arrive in Sherwood, where he had promised to settle his debt.

'Let us go to dinner,' said Big Dick at length.

'Not so,' answered Robin. 'I fear that Our Lady is wrath with me, since she has not sent me my pay!'

'Have no doubts, master!' cried Big Dick. 'It is scarcely noon. Be sure that, before the sun is down, all will come right. I dare be sworn Sir Richard of Legh is true and trustworthy.'

'Then take your bows,' said Robin, 'you and Little Much and Scarlet, and hasten to the Great North Road. And, if the Knight you cannot find, maybe you will meet with another guest to stand proxy for him!'

Off went the three merry men, clad all in Lincoln green with swords at their sides and bows in their hands – but never a sign of Sir Richard could they find.

Presently, however, as they lay in wait behind the bushes, they saw two monks approaching dressed in long black robes and with a large band of serving men and attendants behind them.

52

Then said Big Dick to Little Much, with a broad grin, 'I'll wager my life these monks have brought our pay! So cheer up, loosen your swords in their scabbards, set arrows to your strings – and follow me. The monks have twenty or more followers, I know, but I dare not return to Robin without his expected guests!'

So saying, Big Dick sprang out into the road and was knocked down by a van.

'Look where you're going!' shouted the monk driver.

'I was looking where I was going. I was looking to be knocked down by you!'

'Who is your master?' asked the monk of the figure under the van.

'Who else but bold Robin Hood!'

'He is a strong thief,' quavered the monk, pale with fear. 'I have heard little good of him.'

'You lie!' cried Big Dick, crawling from under the van. 'He is a good yeoman of the forest and he bids you to dinner with him.'

'What if we refuse?' asked the monk.

'Then you'll go bloody hungry,' said Big Dick.

So they brought the two fearful monks to Robin.

'These are your guests,' protested Big Dick.

'This is an outrage,' protested the monk.

'No, it's not,' said Robin, 'it's a dinner. Can't you tell the difference between a dinner and an outrage?'

'I am the Abbot of St Mary's Higher Cellarer, and this reverent monk is my clerk.'

'High Cellarer, ha-ha!' said Robin. 'Then your duty is to supply the Abbey with provisions and wine, and to collect tithes, both in kind and money. Maybe Our Lady has sent me my pay after all, by the hands of this her servant . . . But to dinner first. Big Dick, fill a horn of the best wine for Master Cellarer – who doubtless is an expert on vintages – and let him drink to me!'

So the monks sat with very bad grace. The Cellarer and Master Vintner drank the wine and commented, 'That is fucking terrible.'

'Oh, if you think that's fucking terrible,' said Robin, 'just wait till you taste the grasshopper pie. Now, have you any money to pay for your dinner?'

'I have just written out a cheque for £10,000,' said the Master Vintner.

'Well, make it payable to Robin Hood Enterprises, Charlie Chaplin and Sons,' said Robin. 'That will just about pay for the dinner.'

Just then Sir Richard of Legh came riding hastily to the meeting place.

'Greetings to you, good Knight,' cried Robin, slapping him on the back.

'And good night to you, Robin Hood.'

'What brings you here to Barnsdale, the arsehole of England?' asked Robin.

'My good grace and your kindness and the two and six you lent me. My house and lands are once and for all free of debt. Therefore accept these small gifts. I have brought you a cuddly teddy bear, a quarter-ounce jar of jam, a feather duster, a hundredweight barbell, a ball of wool with knitting needles, a hammer and nails, a fair doll and a large pot of jam.'

The Silver Arrow

10

Tarrah! Boom! Crash! News came to Robin that an archery contest was being held in Cheshire. Oh, who would win? Would it be Robin?

'Oh, Father, Robin will win,' said Maid Marian.

Sir Richard de Custard Kingsley was hosting the tournament. He was doing so, the rumour said, because a dispute had arisen between the foresters of the forests of Delamere and Wirral as to who were the best archers. Oh, oh, oh, will Robin win? It was said the prize was an arrow made of silver with head and feathers of rich red gold.

'I think,' said Robin, 'that we should show Prince John a Sherwood archer could outshoot any contestant put up against them, but first I must have a jam sandwich. As for that silver arrow, I have a great desire to drop it into my quiver.'

'We shall be in great danger,' said Scarlet cautiously from under a table.

Big Dick nodded. 'Maybe our enemies in Nottingham and York will expect Robin to compete for this arrow, and be ready for him should he dare to show himself at this shooting match.'

Robin Hood smiled slowly. 'Exactly,' he said. 'I'll get

in some disguise. Aha, that's it! I'll go as Old Mother Riley.'

'Listen, we can't all go as Old Mother Riley.'

'I'm sorry, but it's Old Mother Riley, and Marian will be Kitty McShane.'

All through the day the competitors shot and shot and many shot each other. Prince John, to increase his popularity among the poorer of the people, was giving free jam sandwiches, a cuddly toy and a weekend in Venice. When the afternoon was far advanced, thirty of the archers lay dead drunk and face down on the ground, leaving only six archers to compete.

'And now,' said Sir Richard de Kingsley, 'since these three are equal (he couldn't count up to six), let them shoot at the eye and that be the final test.'

The first man from Delamere stood forward, gave his long, low cry of 'he, he', knocked his arrow, and drew it to his cheek until the arrow hummed through the air.

Sir Richard stepped down to the target. There was a gasp from the crowd.

'It's in the gold,' he cried, 'but a hair's-breadth out from the eye. Then Delamere has it, unless Sherwood shoot better.'

Once more his bugle rang out and every sound died with the echo of it. Quietly a man from Sherwood took his stand, knocked the arrow (Oh please God, let him win!), glanced down the point at the distant shimmering target, then he drew the mighty bow to its limit. The air seemed to stand still. He let go the bowstring and the arrow sped like a meteor towards the target.

There was a gasp of mingled breath and praise. Richard de Custard Kingsley proclaimed in a great voice, 'I declare that the archer from Sherwood bears away the silver arrow from both Wirral and Delamere. Let the champion, the man of Sherwood, draw near and receive his prize.'

Robin stepped forward.

'Uncover your head, fellow.'

He did, and revealed Old Mother Riley with a feather in her bonnet.

'I bestow this silver arrow upon the best archer present, Old Mother Riley,' announced Sir Richard.

'What is your name, Yeoman?' asked the Prince.

'It's Old Mother Riley. I'm an old cleaning woman from Ireland.'

A Knight dressed in chain mail said, 'This man is not Old Mother Riley; she's in a nursing home in Bognor. That is Robert Fitzooth, truly the Earl of Locksley and an Old Mother Riley impressionist.'

Prince John, putting on his reading glasses, said, 'I'm glad to have seen this far-famed Robin Hood.'

'Shame on you, false Prince,' cried Robin, drawing himself up to his full height and putting on his own glasses. 'This is no way to treat a guest and a lawful winner of a prize.'

'Go in peace, false traitor,' said John, and sang:

We'll meet again
Don't know where
Don't know when

But I know we'll meet again some sunny day
Keep smiling through
Just like you always do
Until we see the dark clouds far away.

'To take Robin Hood here might cause a riot and undo all today's good work but Sir Guy and his men are posted on every road and he cannot escape,' whispered Prince John.

'We are in great danger,' said Robin in a low voice to Big Dick and Scarlet, who were waiting in the crowd. 'Gather the rest of our band and slip quietly away to the north woods where Delamere Forest lies deepest. If they overtake us, fire a volley, then a villey and then a valley and flee into the forest.'

The danger came sooner than Robin had expected. They were not yet out of Kingsley Park when the bushes on every side gave up armed men and the shrill bugle call brought Sir Guy de Custard with several mounted followers galloping straight into the bushes and getting lost.

'Now stand all together, ha, ha,' directed Robin, 'and shoot as you've never shot before – straight. Not one volley, but many, keeping back three or four arrows each. There are but a dozen of us and at least four times that number of them. But wait a minute, ha, ha, has not today shown that the archers of Sherwood surpassed all others?'

'Yield, Robin Hood,' said Guy. 'My men surround you and there's no escape.'

'Aha,' said Robin, 'and this is my answer to you, Sir Guy.'

As he spoke, Robin drew his bow, loosed the arrow from the string and struck Sir Guy de Custard Gisborne on the front of his helmet. It failed to pierce the iron plate but it toppled him backward out of his saddle and brought him to the ground with a crash. His armour weighed two tonnes and they had to wait half an hour while they got a crane to put him back on. In a little while no one durst stand against the archers of Sherwood. They fled in all directions but mostly away.

'Now,' commanded Robin, 'shoot no more but run for the trees where we'll have lunch of porridge sandwiches.'

Guy de Custard had recovered his senses and stapled back the lumps of armour that had fallen off him. He urged on his men while parties kept running in from various glades and clearings in the forest, which were almost continually open in that part – in fact some fell in.

Twice more, bands of men sprang out on Robin and his band in ambush, and just as easily they were wiped out. They were beaten back with quick volleys of arrows.

'Take that, you buggers, ha, ha,' said Robin.

'Look, yonder, the pine-stone house. It's got all mod cons – television, television and TV,' shouted Big Dick.

'Has it a coat of arms?'

'Yes, but no legs.'

It was the house of Sir Richard Legh himself.

'Welcome, its £3.10 a week, B&B. Welcome, welcome,' said Richard, slapping Robin on the back. 'I have a chance of repaying you –' More slapping on the back. 'Kindly be to me what I was to you in Sherwood.' More slapping on the back. 'I bid you and all your men

61

up the drawbridge and fend the walls and the great tower, bolt the doors, the windows, and the cat flap.'

Early next morning came Sir Guy de Custard Gisborne with his armour tied on with string and a large company of men and a fridge, and Richard Legh demanded that he store some beer in the fridge for lunchtime.

'Faugh!' shouted Sir Guy de Custard and, knowing that he had not the means to assault the fortress, he turned for home.

Some days later, with Robin and his men having departed for their forest, Sir Richard's lady mounted her horse and rode day and night until she came to Sherwood.

'God save you, Robin Hood. Sir Guy de Gisborne has, contrary to all law, imprisoned my husband in Nottingham Castle.'

'We can scarce effect a rescue there,' said Robin, looking grave. 'I know: I will wear this model French la femme le frock.'

'I am hees mistress and I needs heem at 'ome,' said the French model, standing on the drawbridge of Nottingham Castle.

As a result of Robin being dressed in a French la femme le frock, Sir Legh of Legh was released from prison and escorted with all honour back to his home.

While Robin was in Nottingham, he discovered that there was a porridge surplus so he smuggled some back in his bra – 33 inches' worth. While dressed like a

Frenchwoman he was arrested by the Sheriff's police for being a lesbian. To prove he wasn't he gave them a photo of his own genitals. They put it on display at the Police Black Museum. Many women asked for a copy.

Robin Hood
And The Butcher

11

Because there was so much to do in Sherwood, some of them did it behind the trees. Nearly all of the food they ate had to be trapped or shot. Alternatively they could buy a pound of sausages, but they were always in danger of sausages being seized by the Sheriff of Nottingham. What with Sir Guy de Custard of Gisborne, and the rest, Robin Hood had to keep five hundred archers on standby. They usually stood by a tree.

On one occasion, Big Dick and Robin were walking by the high road when a cart of meat came jogging along accompanied by a pussy cat who picked up bits that fell off.

'Now then, I've a mind to be a butcher myself. Will you sell me your horse and lend me your pussy cat?' asked Robin.

'Right willingly,' answered the Butcher, and went to bed with a high temperature.

Robin killed the horse (he was a cruel bugger), donned the bloodstained butcher's garb and headed into town with his own horse, followed by the pussy cat.

'Meat to sell! Fresh horse meat to sell! Fresh meat, three pennies a pound and, free for adoption, a pussy cat!'

Among the crowd that gathered round him came the Sheriff's wife and, seeing the meat was good and tender and most unusually cheap, she invited the Butcher to bring his horse, cart and pussy cat to the Sheriff's to sell what was left and then sup with her and the Sheriff.

At dinner, Robin and his cart and his horse learnt many things. He heard that King Richard was a prisoner, and that Prince John was giving it out that he was dead so that he himself might become King.

Next morning Robin was arrested by the RSPCA for cruelty to a horse and having an unlicensed pussy cat. He daren't let on he had another horse in the fridge but was then further arrested by BUPA police for not being ill.

Late that evening the Sheriff asked Robin if he had any horned beasts that he could sell them.

'I can do that,' said Robin, then led the Sheriff and two followers into a herd of three hundred deer on the outskirts of the forest. Robin was easily able to lure them to his forest hideaway.

'You swine of a man. You'll pay for this,' roared the Sheriff.

'No, he's doing it for free,' said Big Dick.

'Fine trade indeed,' announced Robin, pulling a beard and a moustache and an eye patch from his disguise. 'And, see, I've brought with me the Sheriff of Nottingham to dine with us today.'

'He is right welcome,' said Big Dick, 'and I'm sure he will pay well for his dinner.'

'Indeed,' laughed Robin, 'for he has brought some money with him to buy three hundred head of deer from me and already he has offered me a great sum of money to lead him to our secret glade.'

'Are these deer?'

'Yes, very dear. Pound for a pound.'

'By the Rude,' said the Sheriff, shaking with terror, 'had I guessed who you were, a thousand pounds would not have brought me into Sherwood.'

'Oh yes it would. It would also have got you a ticket for Manchester United v Tottenham Hotspur.'

So the Sheriff and his two trembling followers were blindfolded, and they tried, with difficulty, to eat their food. Since all three were blindfolded, Robin feasted them.

Big Dick spread his cloak on the ground and poured into it all the money the Sheriff had brought with him. It came to £500.

'We'll keep their three horses, too,' said Robin, 'and let Master Sheriff and his two men walk back forty miles to Nottingham and a porridge drought. When you next come to visit me in Sherwood,' said Robin quietly, 'you shall not get away on such easy terms. I'll send you all packing back with just your under drawers, ha, ha, ha, ha.'

Then he left them and returned to the secret glade where the Butcher, whose name was Gilbert-of-the-White-Hand, was waiting for him.

'Here are your cart, horse and pussy back again, good Master Butcher. I have had a fine holiday selling meat in your stead – but we must not play too many of such pranks.'

'By the must,' swore Gilbert the Butcher, 'I'll sell meat

no longer if you will have me as one of your merry men. I'll become a vegetarian, and so will my pussy cat.'

That night there was another back-smacking feast. But next day Robin was issued with a summons from the RSPCA for killing a horse. The fine was £10.

Ten pounds! It took three hours to count the money. Tears ran down his cheeks as he counted each pound. He was also fined by BUPA for not being ill.

The Adventures Of The Beggars

12

After Robin's adventure with the Butcher, Gilbert the Whitehand, and his trick played on the Sheriff of Nottingham, Big Dick professed himself to be jealous.

There were in those days a great many beggars wandering about the country. Some were Liberals; some were Conservatives; some of the Green Party; and they were not always either too old or too lame to work. Often, indeed, they were lazy ruffians who only turned up in Parliament for their daily pay. Some were even so lazy they lived on Social Security and Big Macs and chips.

Such a beggar as this, Robin and Big Dick saw striding along the road, waving a great staff in his hand and singing merrily.

'Farewell, Beggar Big Dick,' laughed Robin as he came down the hill. 'There you have your disguise. Hie away to Nottingham and call on the Sheriff!'

'I seem to have lost the first round. But I'll wager you, good master, that I'll bring back better gains as a beggar than ever you would,' said Big Dick.

'Done,' laughed Robin.

Yes, indeed, Big Dick had been done.

'Now I'll hasten after your friend there and see what he has in his bag,' cried Robin.

Away went Robin at his best pace and very soon caught up with the beggar. 'Not so fast there,' shouted Robin, taking out his knife. 'Stand still a minute! Let me see the colour of your gold.'

'Right willing,' answered the beggar. With that he opened the bag and Robin bent down to see what he would take out, the brisk wind ruffling his hair as he did so. The beggar moved round a little so as to get the wind behind him. And then he suddenly pulled out a great handful of ground porridge and flung it into Robin's face.

Robin stowed away his arrows under his coat, unstrung the bow which he could then use as a staff, and set off by the shortest forest paths towards Nottingham. Now he knew there was a porridge surplus. Through the wood he came to the edge of the forest, where he fell off. He came to a crowd clustered around a low knoll on which stood the gallows.

'This is no public spectacle, but a cruel, unlawful wickedness,' said Robin without porridge.

Robin pushed his way right to the front. The crowds were crying shame upon the Sheriff, Prince John, and all Normans – and pity and encouragement to the prisoners. 'Cheer up, you'll soon be dead.'

The Executioner had almost to push his way through the throng. As he passed Robin, he tripped suddenly. Robin uttered a cry, lurched forward as if pushed from behind, and landed on the man's back.

The Captain of the Guard strode forward with several of his men. Roughly they dragged Robin to his feet, and then the Executioner. But the latter fell again for the hot iron in his hand had burnt a great red wound like the letter U on his face – and in falling Robin had broken several of his somethings.

'Your noble worships,' whined Robin, 'the crowd pushed me – I fell – and I broke my something. I could not help it. Spare me, I pray.'

'That's enough grovelling,' said the Prince. 'Fellow, you may go free if you perform the office of executioner in place of the man whom you have injured.'

'Make haste then,' said the Captain. 'There will be trouble if we delay longer.'

'As soon as this iron's white hot,' Robin called out, 'I'll see the right man gets it in the face. Porridge for sale,' he said, 'and one of the condemned men wants to buy some. Mercy, the condemned man wants to eat some porridge. The man's last request – 'tis the law. The other two will have to wait. I'll cook it for him.'

Robin came to the foot of the gallows, raised the iron as if to press the points into the first man's eyes – and then suddenly, twiggerlypoo, straightened himself up and hurled it with dead accuracy into the face of the Captain of the Guard.

'I say, I say, that's jolly unfair,' said the Captain.

The stillness was broken by the scream of pain. During it, Robin flung off the beggar's coat and took up his bow and arrow, ready for action. Robin had his arrow tipped with plague, malaria and typhoid.

'Freemen of England – make way for Robin Hood and his three new followers.'

'Cut him down!' cried the Captain, staggering to his feet. He had to go somewhere.

Robin's bowstring twanged, and the Captain fell to the ground for the last time, an arrow through his heart. He died of plague.

Now the guards made ready as if to attack Robin. But his bowstring twanged twice and two more men lay dead of plague – for at that range even chain mail could not withstand arrows sped by the surest hand that ever plucked a bowstring. Robin loosed one or two more arrows; both guards died of malaria. The remaining guards could only push through the throng slowly. By the time they reached the gallows, Robin and the men he had rescued were lost in Sherwood Forest.

While all this was happening, near Nottingham, where incidentally there had been a porridge glut, Big Dick came late in the afternoon to a fire which had been lit. Around it sat three others. To shorten his temper, a man from the RSPCA wanted to know if he had killed any horses, threatening him with a warrant.

'Greetings, brothers,' said Big Dick. 'I'm glad I've come upon my kind. I hope you've had a better day than I've had.'

Sherwood was still a place of mystery.

Robin Hood
And The Tanner

13

Now then, it was one lovely May day and Arthur the Tanner was singing as he rode. It was bloody awful singing as he went, but he went.

'Well met, jolly fellow, well met,' said Robin, backslapping Arthur. 'You sing like Dorothy Squires. How is the cat skinning going today?'

'Well, I've done 25 cats and some of them have been worn around the neck of highborn ladies, all with flea collars.'

'Now, Tanner, there is a new law. All tanners who drink too much ale and beer are to be set in the stocks. Some will have their legs put in the stocks and their pussy cats' legs too.'

'That's rubbish,' said Arthur, nearly falling off his horse laughing. 'We will not lose any freedom by that, and it will not stop my catching pussy cats. It's a freedom I'll wager that you lose sooner than I do.'

'I'll take your wager, and two cats,' said Robin. 'Let us on to Nottingham. There might be a porridge glut there.'

'But, tell me, what brings you by the forest road?' said Arthur.

'They call it a horse.'

'There is a reward offered for the capture of Robin Hood. I have in my pocket a warrant for his arrest and three cats.'

'If I meet this Robin Hood,' said the Tanner, 'they will pay me a hundred pounds and six cats.'

'Indeed?' mused Robin. He would know more of this grand reward and pussy cats upon his head.

So they went to the inn and Robin had a mead and a matzo; Arthur had an ale and the pussy cats had three coca colas with straws. Bit by bit Arthur became blot-eyed and collapsed to the ground. He was so full he started to leak. Three of the pussy cats escaped from his trouser pocket and ran out of the door shouting, 'Freedom! Freedom! Freedom!'

Robin Hood waited for the drunken slob to recover. He tried to assist him by throwing three bottles of icy water over him. It didn't seem to help so Robin returned to the camp. On the way he adopted three stray pussy cats.

When Arthur the Tanner came to, he was enraged that he had let Robin Hood slip from his fingers, and three cats slip from his trousers. He sprang on his horse and shot off the other side.

Robin returned to the inn and stabled his horse with the stable man. 'It's sixty pence a horse, Robin.'

'Oh look, here's sixty pence and a pound.'

'Why the pound?' said the attendant.

'It's an intelligence test,' said Robin. 'Now pass me the glass. I've just found some water and I want to use it before it goes off.'

So Arthur the Tanner confronted Robin Hood and rushed at him with a good oak staff. WHACK! Down went Arthur. WHACK! Down went Arthur. WHACK! Down went Arthur. WHACK! Down went parts of Arthur. WHACK! Two pieces of Arthur went down. WHACK! Down went some more of Arthur the Tanner.

'And now, there, there, Arthur-a-Whack. Have you had enough?'

'Well, let's put it this way, I don't want any bloody more. You owe me three pussy cats,' said Arthur-a-Whack.

'I'm sorry, I'll set up a pussy cat hunt tomorrow and try and catch them again. Look, Arthur-a-Whack, come and join my merry band in Sherwood Forest, or at least come and dine with us,' said Robin. 'I owe you a good meal in exchange for the thrashing I gave you. You can use as much tomato sauce and jam as you like.'

Robin blew his horn and his socks rolled down. There appeared Big Dick and several others and two cats who were survivors of Arthur-a-Whack.

'By the mass!' exclaimed Arthur. 'Is that Big Dick?'

'That was his name,' answered Robin, 'before a tree fell on him.'

'Big Dick!' said Arthur. 'Big Dick is my own cousin, our mothers being sisters. And I loved him ever since he was a little boy.'

'What is the matter, good master,' called Big Dick as he saw blood on Robin's face.

'Well, that bastard bashed me in the face.'

'Did he? Take that, you bastard!' And he hit Arthur-a-Whack over the head.

'Look, I can't sit here getting bashed. I got to hunt my pussy cats,' moaned Arthur.

A fine dinner was spread before Arthur-a-Whack, and so he became a member of the gang.

Every morning Arthur-a-Whack went riding out looking for pussy cats. He could never see them but they could always see him.

The Wedding Of Allin-a-Dale

14

Robin Hood and his men lived mainly in caves, huts, cupboards, refrigerators and washing machines. They stayed mostly on the tops of trees so they could see other people's heads – many with bald heads, many with grey heads, many with red heads, many unfortunate ones with no heads at all. They lived in the wildest depth of Sherwood Forest and they had many other places as well. There was the basement of the Silver Star Soup Kitchen, the kitchens of McDonald's and Ronny Scott's Hyde Park.

Sir Richard of Legh, the bankrupt Knight whom Robin had saved, had been an ardent follower of King Richard Coeur de Lion. Sir Richard's men were ever ready to shelter Robin Hood. They used an umbrella. They sheltered Robin Hood for nearly six months under the umbrella then they got fed up of holding it.

Robin first saw Allin-a-Dale one spring day as he stood in the pale-green shade of the chestnut waiting to shoot shepherds. When Robin saw him, he'd already killed three and hung them up.

There came the sound of crappy singing and a brave young man came tripping along a forest path and fell flat on his face. He stood up dripping in mud, as fine a sight as could be seen for the perverted. He was clothed in scarlet, red and mud. And, as he strode along, springing a little with each step, he sang as sweetly as a bird. And ever and anon, he paused to strike a trilling melody from the very harp that hung from his shoulder. Clankity clang it went.

Next day Robin saw him again but now he came drooping through the woods, his feet dragging behind him, his head bent. He had caught it in a disco door.

At a sign from Robin, Big Dick and Little Much stepped out into the open and barred the young man's way. But, just to sedate him a bit, Big Dick hit him over the head with a stick and gave him a Valium.

'Stand off, stand off,' cried Big Dick. 'You must come before our master at once.'

'And who is your master?' asked Allin-a-Dale.

'Robin Hood.'

When he was brought before Robin, Robin asked him cautiously, 'Fair sir, have you any cash to spare for my merry men and me?'

'No bloody fear, one's just bashed me over the head.'

'Oh, he was only training,' said Robin.

'I have no money to spare except five shillings and a ring. These I have hoarded for several long years to have at my wedding, but my bride was taken away from me. They are forcing her to marry a grizzled old Knight.'

Awwwwww.

'What is your name?'

'Allin-a-Dale.' Then he sang:

ROBIN HOOD

There'll be bluebirds over
The white cliffs of Dover
Tomorrow just you wait and see.

They went to see bluebirds over the white cliffs but all they saw were sea gulls, a dumped fridge and crows.

'What will you give me, Allin, if I deliver you your true love from the old Knight?' asked Robin.

'Robin, I will swear upon the Bible to be your true and faithful servant and lend you my pussy cat. I'll give you a pound and have the money sent by postal order.'

'But what about these bluebirds over the cliffs of Dover? Will we see them?'

'No, you will see sea gulls, a dumped fridge and crows.'

Robin took the train to Hyde Park and got out. Robin borrowed Allin's harp, wrapped his cloak about him and entered the cathedral where the wedding was being held.

'Oi, you, shitface, where are you going?' said a monk.

'Well,' said Robin, 'first I'm going somewhere to get away from you. I am the best harpist in the North and I'm sure no wedding is complete without music, a cake and a pussy cat.'

'If that is so, you're right welcome, shitface,' said the Bishop. 'Come play to us until the bride and groom arrive.'

We'll meet again
Don't know where, don't know when
But I know we'll meet again some sunny day
Keep smiling through

Like you always do
Till it grew too blue.

The bride came walking down the aisle. She was young but as pale as death and her eyes were red with weeping. After her came the old Knight in a motorised wheelchair. He ran over the bride. He had put a deposit down on her of $10.

Now Robin started to sing louder and louder.

'For God's sake shut up, shitface,' said the Bishop.

'Not so,' answered Robin. 'I see no bridegroom yet for this lovely lass with her youth and beauty. The old man, I suppose her grandfather, comes to give her in marriage to the man of her choice. Is he your choice for the wedding night?' Robin asked the bride.

'No,' she said.

Whereupon the Knight had a heart attack and fell dead at her feet. Robin was quick to pocket the $10. With that, Robin set his horn to his lips and blew out the back of his trousers. Soon the church was live with archers.

'Heel um am,' said Allin-a-Dale.

'So you are,' said Robin.

'Who gives this maid to be married?' asked Big Dick.

'That I do,' cried Robin.

And so, Allin-a-Dale and his bride were married and they had their honeymoon at Sherwood Forest and gave Robin a pussy cat. Gradually Allin's speech became clearer. Unbeknown to all concerned, someone had belted him over the head with a staff.

George-a-Green, The Pinner Of Wakefield

15

Then another forest year went by quickly enough and then it went quicker and reached 92 years early. Robin was getting on a bit now and his hair was growing thin and he was put to wearing a ginger wig and false teeth. Prince John plotted and schemed to gain power and King Richard, after his unsuccessful crusade, was captured by the Archduke of Austria and languished in prison. Blondel, Richard's faithful minstrel, every day tried to haul up to the tower a series of goods – a bottle of Dettol, a tube of Pepsodent and some feather dusters and a box of matches, twenty Players, a cuddly toy, and in case he got lonely a rubber, blow-up woman doll. Blondel sang at the bottom of the tower:

> You are my sunshine my only sunshine
> You make me happy when skies are grey
> You'll never know, dear, how much I love you
> Please don't take that sunshine away.

'For fuck's sake, shut up,' said the voice of King Richard.

The ransom which the Archduke demanded for the

King was £1,000,000. Toward this, Robin sent a pound and asked for a receipt.

George-a-Green had won the world heavyweight wrestling contest and pulled a railway train backwards with his teeth. This last feat was a disaster as all his teeth shot out. George-a-Green's fame, like butter, had spread. He was even mentioned at Bexhill-on-Sea. He had fallen off Mount Everest. He swam the Channel backwards, upside down, and he slew a lion and an elephant, strangled an anaconda, and wrestled with a gorilla. He even slept with the Spice Girls.

Marian took Robin to the side one day. 'Dear heart, one hears so much these days of the deeds and valour of this George-a-Green, and of the beauty of his love for the fair Bettris, who is said to exceed all women in her loveliness. Until recently your name was on everyone's lips and in some people's trouser pockets. And they all sang of you and me, the Queen of Sherwood.'

Now, many evenings later, his cares permitting, George-a-Green walked forth into the country outside Wakefield with Bettris on his arm, to view the fields.

'Tell me, sweet love,' George was saying, 'are you content to wed so simple a man as I when Knights and gentlemen seek your hand in marriage?'

'Oh, George, how can you doubt my love?'

George-a-Green suddenly grasped his staff and flushed with anger as he gazed across the nearest field.

'Look!' he exclaimed. 'There are four men breaking through the hedge. Oh, this is not to be borne.'

'That's it, don't borne it, George.'

'Go back, you foolish travellers! You are wrong – you mustn't borne it!' cried George.

'Are you mad?' cried Robin, who was, of course, the leader of the four.

'No, I'm just having a giddy spell.'

'Look at our limbs,' boasted Robin.

'Sirrah,' answered George, 'the biggest limbs have always got the stoutest hearts. If you are brave men and not cowards, come to me one at a time and I'll trounce you all. I'll stop you borning it.'

'Piss off,' said Robin.

'Sirrah, dare you defy me?' shouted George.

'If we give you a dried fish will you let us go?' asked Will Scarlet.

Then they came together striking mighty blows but by the end it was George who knocked Scarlet a crack on the head and laid him out. They had to send for an ambulance.

'Save your blows for a younger man,' exclaimed Big Dick, and a moment later they too were exchanging blows that rang out like thunder across the peaceful evening fields.

But the end of that round was also that Big Dick felt the Pinner's staff on his head more heavily than his senses could stand. Another ambulance.

'Come on,' cried Robin, taking Big Dick's place, 'spare me not and I'll not spare you. Yes, if you spare me not, I'll spare you not, but if I don't spare you, you'll not spare me.'

Just in case, Robin called the ambulance. They rushed him to hospital where they operated for appendicitis and took him back.

'Ha, ha,' laughed George, equally cornily. 'Make no doubt of that, for I'll be as liberal to you as I was to your friend. In fact, I'll smash your bloody brains in.'

It was a contest with much at stake. Every time Robin hit, he called, 'Cuddly toy, holiday for two in Venice, washing machine, teddy bear, set of dishes.' He never got further – George knocked him down.

So they set to work with great oaken staffs and they were so evenly matched that, though they fought for an hour, neither got in a decisive blow at the other.

'Just wait till I see that cow Marian,' Robin said sotto voce. 'All this mayhem for the love of a bloody woman. I hope she's satisfied,' said Robin with a split head and blood running down his face.

'I'll have that dried fish now,' said George.

Robin was carried back on a stretcher. 'I hope you're satisfied,' he said to Marian.

'Well, you could have come back standing up.'

'I am standing up. I'm just doing it on a stretcher.'

A Night Alarm
And A Golden
Price

16

After spending several days at Wakefield with the merry Pinner George-a-Green and his bonny bride Bettris in the monkey house, they all set out once more for Sherwood. The first day's journey was mainly down the road fighting the monkeys off. A monkey and a dozen men at arms swung round a corner in front of them at a trot and came past before they had any chance of hiding.

The Knight did not stop but his visor was down, which caused him to keep riding into trees and houses.

'Walk on,' said Robin quietly to his men. 'Try and ignore the monkeys but follow me quickly and quietly into the wood as soon as they are out of sight. That was Sir Guy de Custard of Gisborne – who is my sworn enemy.'

'What is he doing with that monkey?' asked Marian.

'He's taking it for a walk.'

'Where are you leading us?' George said at last.

'To seek shelter for the night and give your monkey a rest.'

'Whither go you, my masters?' asked Big Dick. 'There be rogues in that direction.'

'Can you show us any direction in which there are no rogues?' said Robin.

'Yonder.' He pointed to a door invitingly open and on the threshold was Arthur-a-Whack.

'Welcome, welcome, good Robin Hood!' cried Arthur, and slapped him on the back, arousing all those painful bits. 'And welcome to your brave followers. My wife and I are indeed honoured by your company.'

'Now don't overdo it. I fear that we bring danger with us,' said Robin, 'and a monkey.'

They came to the great stone-flagged room which served as kitchen and hall, and indeed the whole ground floor of the little house was all in one. So was Robin and so was Marian and Arthur-a-Whack and his wife and a monkey. They were all in one.

And, when he had introduced George and Bettris, they all sat down on rough-hewn benches which gave them numerous splinters in the bum.

'Ah, this wine is Sancerre,' said George.

'No, frog wine,' said Arthur.

Even as he said this, his wife caught him suddenly by the arm and pointed to the window. Outside there was an armed Knight with plumes tossing in the storm. Alas, with the torrential rain his plumes all hung down, blinding him.

'Shelter for a poor traveller who has lost his way in the storm!' came a voice from outside.

'Who and what are you? What identity have you?'

'We are soldiers taking a poor monkey for a walk.' And they put the monkey through the letterbox.

'Are you alone?' said Robin.

'Not with a monkey.'

Back came the monkey through the letterbox.

In the end there was an angry, 'Look, if you don't let us in I will break my fist down on this door.'

'Aha,' said George-a-Green, 'we are ready for you. You thought to rob, murder and set a monkey on my monkey. Well, we're ready for you. We must warn you that we have a jar with leprosy spores in it and, the moment you come in, we'll break it.'

Then Robin, Scarlet, Big Dick and George drew back to the other end of the room and the door gave a crash and a dozen or more armed men were seen in the opening followed by a monkey. The instant the door broke, the five bows twanged and as many arrows rushed unerringly to their marks. Five soldiers lay dead on the floor. Arthur then picked up the leprosy spores and threw them at the Captain of the Guard.

'Help,' screamed the Captain, 'I've got leprosy.'

And then, 'Mercy, good sir,' gasped the Knight. 'Put down your swords, men: we are fairly beaten.'

'Guy of Gisborne, you shit,' said Marian, flinging back her hood so he could see who had defeated him.

'I've got a good idea: let's chop off his head,' said Robin, so chip, chop and off it came.

The next morning they set off again for Sherwood.

'I hope there're no more adventures before we are safe in our own glades,' said Robin.

'Yes, as long as you don't go near any rivers,' said George.

'Shoosh,' cautioned Robin. 'Come quietly hither behind these bushes, good George, and I believe that you will see how we gather our tithes in Sherwood Forest. Yes, the good Friar is collecting subscriptions for King Richard's ransom!'

The travellers saw Friar Tuck, his mighty quarterstaff in his hand, talking with two trembling priests.

'Alas, we have not so much as a penny piece between us. For this very morning we met with robbers who took from us everything we had, including our pile ointment.'

'Stand, base Friar!' roared Robin.

Friar Tuck looked up. 'Robin Hood, forever my master,' went on the grovelling cur.

'Any news?'

'Yes, a man from the RSPCA has heard you are in possession of some monkeys and wants to know if they're being well looked after. A verger brought you a six-pound tin of jam and you'll be delighted to know that we've eaten it.'

'And look what I bring with me,' answered Robin. 'Brave George-a-Green, the Pinner of Wakefield, who is now one of us, and with him his bride, the lovely Bettris, who has brought us another six-pound pot of jam.'

Jam, jam wonderful jam
I will eat it where'ere I am

So they sat down to a feast of six pounds of jam and for days afterwards they were stuck to each other.

The Witch Of Paplewick

17

'Can I come in or are Jews excluded?' The voice came from a man with a black moustache called Groucho.

'Welcome to Sherwood Forest,' said Robin.

'And you're welcome to it, too,' said Groucho. 'As a matter of fact, if this is Sherwood Forest I can't see the wood for the trees.'

One summer's day Robin Hood decided to hold yet another boring feast to entertain the shepherds. Unfortunately, this was a sad occasion, for Eglamour had lost his love, Earine.

'Lost? Hasn't he looked for her?' said Groucho. 'Was she insured?'

'Yes, but they only paid out fifty pounds.'

'You couldn't afford to bury her in the ground with that. You'll have to bury her above ground.'

Eglamour would not believe she was dead but sought her still by wood, by woe, by telegraph, by telephone, by telex, by lighthouse.

'My Marian,' cried Robin.

'Robin, my love!' she answered. 'Oh, now my day's happiness is complete. I rose early, early before the sun, and such fine sport we had seeking the deer. Then one shot brought him down.'

'Yes, nothing like killing deer to start a happy day,' said Groucho.

'Only one shadow fell upon us,' said Marian. 'When we had killed the deer and cracked it up, a raven sat in a tree over our heads and croaked.'

'You say he croaked?' said Groucho. 'He's lucky to be alive.'

'They are wise birds and know that it is ever the huntsman's custom, when he cleaves the brisket bone, to set aside the spoon of it with the gristle that grows there – which indeed is often called the Raven's Bone. [Mrs Beaton, p. 141.]

'The Mother Maudlin, the Witch of Paplewick, can take any form she will and fill them in. She can even become a pot of jam,' said Marian.

'Yes, the witch,' said Groucho, 'by her wobbling I'd say she needed a slimline aerodynamic broomstick.'

Groucho fired an arrow into the air on the off chance it would fall on somebody. There was a loud explosion. By a lucky chance he'd hit a taxi, puncturing the driver.

'How now, sweet Marian?' began Robin. 'Shall we to the feast?'

'Feast!' cried Marian, her voice filled with anger. 'What bloody feast?'

'Why, your bloody feast,' said Groucho.

'Why, Marian, how strange you look,' said Robin.

'Oh, I am well,' snapped Marian.

'There, let us call our friends to the feast.'

'Yes, let us. I'm one,' said Groucho. 'I'll see if I'm in.'

'Friends,' cried Marian, whirling her rosary round and

round her head. 'They shall not feast on this venison. Scarlet, take up the venison – swiftly now! Carry it to Mother Maudlin, the wise woman whom you call a witch, and her white crow. Mr Marx is keen to know if it's changed colour.'

'If it's green now it's a parrot,' said Groucho.

'Marian, can this be true?' gasped Robin.

'I think she's running out of her tablets,' said Groucho.

'Am I dreaming that I am now Robin Hood and this is Marian?' said Robin.

'You are Robin Hood right enough, you grovelling little creep,' said Groucho.

Marian left with Will Scarlet and the feast.

'I fear she is stricken with some illness,' said Robin at last.

'It's Alzheimer's disease,' said Groucho.

Suddenly Marian appeared. 'Robin, xypta monzal prup a pool.'

'That's Alzheimer's! I'd recognise it anywhere,' said Groucho.

'Yes,' Robin proclaimed. 'I want you to see a London psychiatrist. I'll get it on BUPA.'

'Look, here comes Big Dick.'

'Good master,' he called, 'here is Mother Maudlin. She says that she comes in gratitude with some gift made by Maid Marian.'

Alas, although Eglamore had rediscovered his lost love, the witch cast a spell on Will Scarlet and he became a frog.

'Mind how you tread,' said Groucho.

The witch turned and sped away swiftly on her broomstock to a holiday in Japan at Karaoke Holiday Camp. Now that Earine had been discovered alive, there was no reason she couldn't eat a Big Mac and chips.

And still, Sherwood was a place of mystery.

The Last Of Guy
Of Custard
Gisborne

18

The last Guy of Custard Gisborne
Now take thou gold and fee
Sir Guy will come and moat thou be
Your rear will go numb
So he gets kicked right up the bum.
Anon, 'Folk Play of Robin Hood', before 1476

It was a glorious spring morning. Groucho was sipping oxygen through a straw. New leaves were fully opened and so were all the pubs. The greenwood was all fresh and daisy-clad, and the birds sang merrily in every tree.

Loudest of all sang the thrush. Robin shot it.

'Let us go and see if there is a porridge surplus in Nottingham,' he cried.

Off went Big Dick whistling happily but, alas, he came upon two dead men with arrows in their hearts and it needed only a glance to tell him that both these fellows were outlaws and members of Robin's band.

'Aren't you going to call the police?' asked Groucho. 'It's a case of double homicide here.'

Will Scarlet came hopping down the road for his life.

William Trent, whom Big Dick knew well and had once thrashed at quarterstaff, stepped up on to a log and loosed his arrow, and Will Scarlet pitched forward on to his face.

'How do you bury a frog?' asked Groucho.

'It were better for you, William Trent, that your hand had been smitten off at the wrist 'er you fired that shot,' cried Big Dick, and as he spoke his bow twanged and Will Scarlet's slayer lay dead.

'They're dropping like flies around here,' said Groucho. 'Soon we won't have enough characters left to finish this story!'

The Sheriff's men were upon Groucho and bound him.

'I'm on a goodwill visit to Nottingham to see if there's any chance of a porridge surplus,' he cried.

The Sheriff rode up and surveyed Big Dick. 'You shall be drawn at rope's end by down and dale back to Nottingham and then hanged on Castle Hill.'

'Not much of an offer,' said Groucho. 'Get a solicitor. He'll have you off in a day. He'll have you bankrupt in an hour and a half. I'll send a fax to Robin to tell him.'

Fax
Big Dick preparing for death. Seek advice.
PS: No porridge surplus in Nottingham.

Meanwhile, Robin was speaking to a forester who had a duck on a lead.

'You carry in your hand a fine bow. I presume you're a good archer,' said Robin.

'No, I'm a bloody awful one.'

'Come with me then and bring your duck.'

'I wish to meet Robin Hood,' said the stranger, 'and I would fain be one of his company.'

'We'll shoot at that white patch of lichen – that will make a bull's eye,' suggested Robin.

Robin aimed carefully at the mark. He missed.

With that he flung down his bow and quiver and stomped off. The stranger called Robin when he had gone a dozen yards. Now his voice had changed. Robin spun round at the sound of his voice; round and round and round he went. He recognised the voice as that of Sir Guy de Custard Gisborne.

The staples and string which once repaired his armour now held his head in place.

'This is the last round,' said Guy grimly, and very slowly drew back the string of his bow to point at Robin's heart.

'Look out, you'll kill the duck! To shoot an unarmed man is shame indeed and damnation to the fellow,' cried Robin.

Guy de Custard flushed a little at Robin's words and said, 'Indeed, when Robin of Locksley became Robin Hood of Sherwood he was cast out beyond the law of man and beyond the pale of honour. In a little while I shall wind my horn and thereby the Sheriff shall know that Robin is dead.'

'I prefer peanut butter on matzos,' said Groucho.

As he spoke, with a sudden movement Robin flung the knife which he held in his hand and flung himself forward on the ground with the same movement.

'That's the finest draw I've seen since Wild Bill Hickok shot Billy the Kid. You need an agent,' said Groucho.

A moment later Robin, on his feet again, his sword drawn in his hand, charged down upon Guy.

'I think he's coming your way, Guy,' said Groucho.

'I'll take possession of this duck; his life is in mortal danger,' cried Robin.

With that Robin smote off Guy's head.

'I always said you'd get ahead,' said Groucho.

Some time later Robin was walking through the forest wearing Sir Guy de Custard Gisborne's armour.

'Yonder he comes,' cried the excited Sheriff. 'Come hither, good Sir Guy, and ask of me any reward you will.'

'As I have slain the master, give me the man to slay as and when I will.' And, turning quickly, Robin pointed to Big Dick, who now lay bound.

'A mad choice when gold might have been yours for the asking,' said the Sheriff.

Suddenly a Knight clad from head to foot in black armour and riding a great black horse came riding up the road.

'Back, you damned wolves!' cried the Black Knight. 'I cannot see four men borne down by such a host. Charge, foresters! St George for merry England and three pence off income tax!'

At this unexpected attack many of the Sheriff's men broke and fled. The Black Knight paused only for a moment to shout, 'Stay, you base curs! Or I'll beat you back to your kennels.'

'Just you watch out, you guys. He's not joking,' said Groucho.

The Silver Bugle
And The Black
Knight

19

High deeds achieved by knightly fame
From Palestine the champion came
The cross upon his shoulders born
Battle and blast had dimmed and torn
Each dint upon his battle shield
Was token of a foughten field
           Sir Walter Scott, *Ivanhoe*, 1820

The news of a shooting match was one thing sure to draw Robin Hood out of Sherwood. Robin set forth for Ashby-de-la-Zouche in Leicestershire.

'You're doing this for her?' said Groucho.

A great tournament was being held there by Prince John. The danger to Robin was as great as when he had won his silver arrow. But he had pawned that. Prince John, though his power had greatly increased, was by no means accepted as King of England. There were rumours that Richard was free.

The main feature of the tournament was, of course, the jousting Knights who had to knock each other out of the saddle.

All that morning the battle raged and Sir Wilfred, who was the victor, fainted when the crown of victory was placed over his head – it was too big by far and slipped over one eye.

When the time came for the archery contest, all of the marksmen stepped forward, Robin amongst them. Prince John immediately recognised Robin, but was no more able to apprehend the outlaw in the midst of this tournament than he was at the last.

'You dare to show your face here!' roared the Prince. 'You dog, you-you-you . . .'

'Don't call me a you-you,' interrupted Robin. 'Locksley is my name, if you please, Your Highness.'

'It does not please me,' spluttered Prince John.

'Bollocks then,' said Robin.

One by one the archers stepped forward and each discharged their arrows. Most failed to hit the distant target. Only two landed in the gold. One was fired by Robin and the other was shot by a certain Hubert.

'As far as anybody is listening, I think Robin's going to win. I've got one hundred to one on him,' said Groucho.

'How, Locksley, will you match your skill against Hubert?' sneered the Prince.

'Many a good bow was drawn on Senlac Field,' answered Robin. 'But only one side shot their arrows at random into the air, and it was such an arrow that struck King Harold in the eye.'

'Eh?' said the Prince.

'This is no fair match you propose,' said Robin. 'Do you shoot first, friend Hubert?'

Hubert loosed an arrow which flew straight and true to the edge of the gold.

'You have not allowed for the wind, Hubert, or that would have been a better shot!' said Robin.

Thus encouraged, Hubert set another arrow to the string and, taking the light breeze into account, his shaft struck the target exactly in the centre.

'Oh, fuck,' said Robin. 'I've gotta do better than that.'

The duck followed Robin to his mark. 'I will notch his shaft for him, however,' muttered Robin. He let his arrow fly. It stuck right upon that of his competitor, which it split to shivers.

'And now, Your Highness,' said Robin quietly, 'I crave permission to plant such a mark as we use in Sherwood.'

'Quack, quack,' went the duck.

'Stop that! This is serious stuff,' said Groucho.

With that, Robin and his duck walked to the nearest picket and returned with a willow wand six feet long, perfectly straight and not much thicker than a man's thumb. This he peeled, remarking as he did so that it was an insult to ask such a fine archer as Hubert to shoot at a target which might just as well have been a haystack in a farmer's field.

'But,' he concluded, as he went and stuck the willow wand in the ground and returned to Prince John, 'he that hits yonder rod at a hundred yards, I call him an archer fit to bear bow before any king – even before our good Richard of the Lion Heart himself.'

'Cowardly dog!' fumed Prince John. He spat and his teeth shot out. 'Well, Locksley, you split that wand.'

'I will do my best,' answered Robin.

So saying, he again bent his great bow, putting one foot on the duck to steady himself, but on the present occasion looked with care to his weapon, then took aim very slowly and deliberately, and loosed while the waiting multitude held their breath. The arrow sped towards its target and split the willow wand, and a great roar of applause rose.

'Robin, you need an agent. My card, and you just won me $800.75,' said Groucho.

'Well, Locksley, you have made true your boast,' grumbled the Prince, 'and here is the silver bugle horn filled with Mars bars and Dairy Delight ice cream.'

'Thank you,' said Robin.

The Prince said, 'Go in peace now – but remember that I have sworn vengeance on you and your duck.'

'Right,' said Robin. 'Would you like a Mars bar?'

'Yes.'

'I thought you would, you bastard.'

'Oh,' said Maid Marian, 'oh, Robin, you've won. I knew you would.'

'And I've just made $800.75,' said Groucho.

'You know that yonder braggart archer is none other than Robin Hood?' grumbled the defeated Hubert.

'Yes, I know that yonder braggart archer is none other than Robin Hood. But you know I'm none other than the famous Groucho Marx and I'm $800.75 richer.'

As they were returning through Sherwood to the secret glade, Robin met the Black Knight.

'All right, Black Knight,' said Robin, 'if any danger

threatens you, noble sir, know that I or any of my men will come at once to your aid.'

'Well, my main danger comes from my bank manager and my overdraft,' said the Black Knight.

'We are keeping dangerous company,' said Robin, a bankrupt. 'I see the flash of armour behind the bushes.'

'Oh, a flasher,' said Maid Marian, 'a flasher and in Sherwood.'

Without a moment's hesitation the Black Knight set spurs to his horse and charged in the direction of the bushes. He was met by six or seven well-armed men. The Black Knight immediately chopped them all off. The armless men tried to ride their horses home and went in all directions.

'Come with us, good Knight,' begged Robin.

'Are you saying good night or good Knight?' said Groucho.

'Come now, good Knight. You will dine with us and we will entertain you. First you will have a vindaloo porridge.'

Robin Hood
And The Tall
Palmer

20

There'll be blue birds over
The white cliffs of Dover
Just you wait and see

I waited to see and all we saw were sea gulls, a dumped fridge and crows.

One day the Bishop of Peterborough craved an audience with Prince John. The Bishop was fearful to venture forth near Sherwood lest he be molested by Robin Hood.

'My Lord,' said the Bishop, 'I have but a small company.'

'Can you buy shares in it?' asked Groucho.

'My Lord, Sherwood is beset with outlaws. I must claim protection. I need a Centurion tank.'

On the hillside outside Nottingham, a tall palmer sat on his horse. Under his palmer's robe he wore a shirt and leggings of chain mail; on his head under the palmer's hood was a skullcap of steel. He wore a pair of jockey

123

pants and a vest. In his backpack he had three bottles of tomato sauce which he kept for his defence. He would open one over his victim, who would then think they were bleeding to death.

Presently a man came across the fields. Mind you, he'd come across before. The Palmer spoke a few words to the messenger, who saluted and gave himself a black eye.

Soon the Bishop of Peterborough and his Centurion tank came slowly down the hill. The Palmer rode forward and saluted him humbly.

'My lord, I beg to ride with you through the forest. I hear there are outlaws and I would be safer with you inside your Centurion tank.'

'You are most welcome,' answered the Bishop. 'I fear greatly my men would afford small protection should Robin Hood attack. That is why we have this Centurion tank.'

'Yes, do you have any cats?' said the Palmer.

'Yes, I have one back at the monastery. Why?'

'I collect homeless cats.'

'But he isn't homeless.'

'Well, if you threw him out the cat flap he would be.'

'Yes, I suppose that would be one way of making him homeless.'

Through the leafy trees the Bishop could see half a dozen men busy skinning and cutting up a newly slain deer.

The Bishop stood up. 'How dare you kill the King's venison, contrary to the forest laws?'

'We are shepherds. Today we have decided to make merry and have killed this fine, fat deer for our dinner.'

'Impudent fellow, you shall go to Prince John, who usually hangs deer slayers for the first offence.'

'Oh mercy,' cried the Shepherd.

'No mercy,' replied the Bishop.

The Shepherd drew a horn from his coat and blew three notes upon it.

The Bishop sat gaping. Suddenly there came running foresters.

'What is your will, good master?' said Big Dick, bending a little before the leading shepherd.

'Here is the Bishop of Peterborough in a tank. He proposes to hang us all and he will grant us no mercy.'

'Cut off his head, master,' said Big Dick, 'and bury him under this tree.'

'Oh mercy, mercy,' cried the Bishop, trembling inside his Centurion tank, for he now recognised the leading shepherd as Robin Hood.

The lid of the Centurion tank opened and out stepped the Palmer. 'I think this is where we part company, Bishop. Good Robin Hood,' he said, 'I am not of this man's party, but I cannot sit and see a bishop done to death without raising a hand to help him. I have fought in the Holy Land with Richard in the crusade against the infidel Saracens.'

'Good Palmer,' answered Robin courteously, 'with you I have no quarrel. But come with us now and taste our hospitality. Only justice shall be done. But first you will swear.'

'I swear. I also drink and smoke.'

'May I give you this gift of three tomato-sauce bottles as a sign of my friendship?' said Robin.

'If I had a friend like that I'd shoot him,' said Groucho.

'Robin will be back soon, Bettris,' said Marian.

Bettris suddenly stopped and gazed fixedly at the bracken.

'What is it, Bettris?' asked Marian.

'I thought I saw a face, there in the ferns,' answered Bettris. 'Yonder! Yes, they are shaking still.'

'You know that fern shaking is forbidden in Sherwood,' said Groucho.

Even as she spoke the bracken parted and Prince John strode into the glade and slid on a banana.

Marian whispered to Bettris, 'He slipped on a banana. Let's wait and see what he does next.'

'So here's the tigress in her den!' cried Prince John. 'Marian, after all these years we meet again.'

'No, we are vegetarians. We'll never have meat again.'

'Come, there is no escape,' sneered Prince John. 'Our horses wait beyond the rocks with the good forester who tracked you down at last.'

'Just wait till I see him. I'll set fire to his wedding tackle,' said Groucho.

'Robin will save us!' cried Marian.

'I'm afraid Robin Hood is too busy getting the Bishop of Peterborough out of his vegetarian Centurion tank,' replied Prince John.

Marian stepped backward and fell over. Quickly she took a horn from her belt and blew the Wa-sa-hoa call on it. Then she snatched up the sword which Bettris had brought her and stood on the defensive.

'Quick,' she said, 'more bananas.'

And Bettris immediately threw one dozen bananas in the middle of all the horsemen, whose horses slipped all over the place, and they slid off their mounts, peeled them and ate them. It was a good ploy by Marian but not clever enough. Some of the horses fell over, but not all.

The three surviving men at arms, seeing Robin's men returned, suddenly ran for their lives. But not far – several arrows came from among the trees on either side and they lay dead long before they reached another banana. The Prince and the Bishop were captured.

'Now,' said Robin, 'the Bishop of Peterborough has been brought to dinner in a Centurion tank. Let us see what appetites you have.'

'You live well, friend Robin Hood.'

Commercial
Ariel is the washing powder for you.
It washes clean; Maid Marian uses no other.

[I will come back to the second half of this commercial break later on in the story.]

'In that,' answered Robin, 'I hold that we break no just law. But I hold that we are not outlawed lawfully. It's John's doing and that of the minion of the Sheriff of Nottingham. We dwell here to set right the wrong; never yet did we hurt any man knowingly who was honest and true, but only those who – with or without the law on their side – robbed innocent men or oppressed them, or did ought against the honour of a woman. They call me the poor man's friend!

127

'Come now, good master Palmer – we are at least thieves of honour, and you do no dishonour, that is unless you shrink from eating the King's deer.'

'Shrink?' The Palmer laughed heartily. 'Ha, ha ha. I am as hungry as if I had walked all the way home from Jerusalem – and as thirsty, too.'

When the meal was ended, Robin turned to the Bishop.

'My lord,' he said gravely, 'you have dined with me this day from the inside of a Centurion tank. Come, drink with us to King Richard and then pay us and be gone. Now, Bishop, have you anything with you in that Centurion?'

'But little. Two hundred pieces of ammunition.'

'Just pass it through the hatch. Thank you. I'll send them to the German Army.'

'I know not what I have,' said the Palmer. 'Sometimes it is much; sometimes it is little; sometimes it is bugger all.'

'Since you say bugger all,' replied Robin, 'not a penny will I touch. You shall play our game of buffets but first the Bishop will dance a jig for us.'

And the Bishop was forced to pull up his skirts and dance a jig, whether he would or not, while all the outlaws roared (with forced laughter) at his comical fat figure and angry red face.

'Red is funny, Robin? So far your games are a total pain in the arse,' said Groucho.

'Enough, enough,' panted Robin, 'we have had sport enough of this kind. Now our game of buffets.'

'How is that played?' asked the Palmer.

'Simple,' said Robin. 'It's a game for oafs. Stand up and receive a buffet from us and, if it fails to knock you down, you will give out a buffet in return.'

'A fine sport, truly,' said the oaf, Big Dick, and forthwith he bared a forearm that any smith might have been proud of.

'Come on, Big Dick,' said Robin, 'and show this man that all the men of metal are not away crusading.'

Big Dick, like a true oaf, rolled up his sleeve, drew back his arm and threw a mighty buffet. The Palmer seemed scarcely to notice it. Instead he raised his arm and sent Big Dick on the turf.

'Have I now paid for my dinner, good Robin?' he asked.

'You must be the strongest oaf I've met,' replied Robin.

So Prince John was led out of the cave where he had been left, and sat down before Robin Hood. The tall Palmer saw him and uttered an exclamation. He threw back his hood.

The Palmer looked Prince John full in the face, which fell off, and he turned a ghastly colour, khaki, and fell grovelling at the Palmer's knees.

'Richard!' he gasped. 'King Richard, my brother.'

'Loose his bonds,' commanded the King. He had about 150 of them invested in stock in America.

Prince John stood to his feet, reeling and ghastly pale. His horse was brought to him. It kicked him in the balls, ran over him and galloped wildly away.

King Richard turned to Robin, who knelt before him, speedily followed by all the outlaws. 'Pardon, my Liege.'

'He didn't recognise you the first time, King,' said Groucho.

'Stand up again,' said the King, raising Robin. 'Stand up, my friend. I freely pardon you and all here present. You and your doings are spoken of throughout England . . .'

'He's been robbing and killing for years and all you've heard about are his doings?' said Groucho.

'. . . and that Lady Marian lives still a maid until I, the King, join you both in marriage. Is this true?'

'It is, my Liege,' answered Robin.

'I'm not a liege. I am a king.'

And Marian came and slipped him a ham sandwich.

'Married you shall be,' said the King. My Lord of Peterborough shall join your hands in holy matrimony. And that good deed shall wipe out what is past.'

So they drove to their honeymoon, which they had at Ronny Scott's. They had to wait until the place had emptied out at three o'clock in the morning.

The Sheriff fled the country. 'He's off to see his rabbi.'

'I didn't know he was Jewish,' said Groucho.

'Yes, he is.'

'How do you know?'

'I saw him in the shower.'

King Richard didn't remain long in England; the overdraft was killing him. The archers became soldiers to King Richard, and they went overseas. They were remembered only in the songs which the minstrels were singing of Robin Hood and his merry men.

In the honeymoon bed, Robin took his duck. It would be a great strain on the marriage.

Robin Hood's Last Adventure

21

Robin Hood rode for the coast, to Scarborough, to escape Prince John, who was worse than ever with his brother away again. He bought a fish and found lodgings with a fishwife. She was lamenting she was a poor fishwife. She had to cook all the fish that the fishermen caught. This time they had caught a shark and half of the crew was in it.

'My husband is *still* in it,' she said.

Robin found the shark hanging up in the harbour. 'Anyone in there?' he shouted.

'Yes. I'm the fishwife's husband. Could you help get me out?'

Eventually he found his way out and emerged covered in fish oil. He gave Robin a fish.

Then Robin joined a fisherman's ship and, whereas the fishermen used a huge net, Robin, not easy in the ways of fishermen, shot a fish at a time with an arrow. At the end of the day the fishermen had caught half a ton and he had caught three fish.

One day the Captain gave a shout of 'Ahoy, pirates!' Sure enough, there were Ahoy, pirates. Robin Hood held them off with his bow and arrow. Then he gave a loud call with his horn and soon his archers came and they shot the shit out of the pirates. Alas, the archers did not know how to sail a ship so it sank from neglect. Robin gave the fishwife a single fish for his rent.

'Welcome home, Robin. I thought you had saved a fish for me,' she said.

The Pope wrote a note to Marian: '*No tocca tua corpo*', meaning 'Don't let any scheming bastard touch your body'.

The Last Arrow

22

Weep ye woodmen wail
Your hands with sorrow ring
Your master Robin Hood lies dead,
Poor old thing. Hey ding a ling.

William J MacGonigal

At Short and Curly's Nunnery the Prioress welcomed Marian and led her at once to sanctuary.

Several days later Prince John's men came to the nunnery demanding that Marian should be given up to them.

The Prioress refused. 'The Lady Marian has taken sanctuary and she has crabs,' she said, 'and not the King himself can touch her now. I have my love for Robin Hood and, were it he and not his wife who knelt with hand on the altar, he were yet inviolate.'

But when they had gone she spoke with Marian many times.

'Good daughter,' she said, 'I have certain news that Robin Hood has snuffed it. Moreover, though I will withstand him to the last, King John may yet take you hence by force.'

137

So the Prioress exhorted Marian until Marian believed indeed that Robin was dead. And so she asked nothing better than to take the veil and pass the rest of her days in prayer to God, tending the sick, the lepers, and just hoping she didn't get it. When Prince John came Marian just pole vaulted him until he left.

At long last Robin Hood came. He came leaning on a stick, an old, sick man with a dried fish, though he was not much more than forty. He had limped his way painfully across country to Short and Curly's, growing rapidly weaker and more in debt as he went. And now he knocked at the door and begged the Prioress's aid.

'Come in, good sir,' said the Prioress gently. 'Here you are, have a nice jam sandwich. And she led him to a room on the ground floor at forty shillings a week. It looked out towards Sherwood. Then she put Robin to bed and opened a vein in his arm to let blood, which was considered at the time to be one of the cures for illness.

'Which one of you is Dracula?' said Groucho.

Presently Robin recovered a little, sat up and fell back.

'Good Mother Prioress,' he said, 'I must speak with you.'

'Speak, son. God alone will hear what you tell.'

'Not too fast: he's bottoming out,' said Groucho.

'Then know,' said Robin, 'I am Robert Fitzooth Locksley, Earl of Huntingdon. I had a million pounds in the Midland Bank. Every coin was proudly stolen.'

The Prioress stirred suddenly. Nothing happened but it happened suddenly.

'Good Mother Prioress, months ago my Marian and I fled from Nottingham. We could not escape together.

Only I could escape together, and she had to escape together on her own. Have you news of my wife?'

'She came here.'

'Ah, then, she must be here,' cried Robin, trying to rise from his bed.

'When you are better.'

'Could I have a jam sandwich?' asked Robin.

'Yes. Sleep now and tomorrow you can travel to see her. I will lend you a horse, and two of my serving men shall ride with you.'

'Yes, but she's here,' said Robin.

'Yes, yes, they will bring you back here,' said the Prioress.

As soon as she was certain he was sleeping, the Prioress loosened the bandages on his arm so the blood flow increased. She then stole quietly away.

All day Robin lay there bleeding slowly.

'You're bleeding slow,' said a nun.

'He's going as fast as he can,' said Groucho. 'In fact, he's nearly empty.'

He was so weak now that he could hardly move. He saw the bandage had been unfastened purposely and he guessed that the Prioress had done it.

Robin staggered to his feet, flung open the window, and fell out and had to be dragged back in. But he could not raise a leg to get it over. Then he thought of his bugle horn. With trembling fingers he drew it from his pouch, and blew the old horn, 'Wa-sa-hoa'.

Out in the forest Big Dick heard it. 'That was Robin's horn, but I fear my master is near to death, he blows so wearily.'

He hastened to the nunnery with a stretcher and an accompanying coffin.

The notes came to Marian's ears from nearby. She had in fact got nearby ears. She sprang to her feet. 'Oh, my Robin, my love, my love,' she cried. She ran to the room where the sound was coming from.

'Marian,' he whispered, 'they told me you'd been appearing in cabaret at Stringfellow's.'

'It was only one week,' she said.

Then Marian told him what had happened to her and all her adventures.

'Listen, this guy's bleeding to death,' said Groucho.

'Here have I come to die and where else can I ask but in your arms?'

'Well, you could have done it at Stringfellow's.'

By this time Big Dick had broken into the room and was weeping at Robin's side. 'Oh, my master, my master,' he sobbed. 'Grant my one last wish. Let me burn Short and Curly's Nunnery and slay the wicked Prioress.'

'No, never,' said Robin, 'that is a boon I will not grant you. Never in my life did I hurt a woman or a kangaroo, nor raise my hand against a maid or a plumber. Nor shall it be done at my death. Do not blame the Prioress for my death and my overdraft. First give me my bent bow and set an arrow on the string. Where the arrow falls, there bury me.'

He took aim and the arrow landed on the roof of a police car. So, whenever a police car goes by, Robin is buried in the roof.

Marian came first in the nuns' pole vault. Sometimes,

at the top of a vault, she could see Robin go by in a police car. When Robin was fed up being dead in the police car and missing his Weetabix, the ideal breakfast food and lovely with cold milk, he came down and took Marian to London. He booked two cheap day returns and took her to Ronny Scott's.

When he went to heaven St Peter wouldn't let him in, so Robin shot him in the leg.

'You swine, Robin. That's my good leg.'

Then Jesus came and, with a miracle at the feast, turned St Peter from water into wine.

'Now clear off, Robin,' he said, and confiscated his bow.

So Robin cleared off back to Ronny Scott's, where he sang jam-sandwich blues. Everything went OK except Robin didn't like one of the waiters and shot him in the leg.

'Ah, I know someone who can mend that,' he said, and took him to Jesus, who mended it but charged him a pound.

'Look, running heaven is expensive. Keeping the Jews in fried fish costs one hundred pounds a year.'

'I'll fix that,' said Robin, and shot several people in the leg.

Jesus healed them all and collected £100.

'You're great, Robin. I'll keep you on as Holy Resident Archer.'

But Robin longed for the old days in Sherwood with Marian pole vaulting, so he returned to robbing the rich. He held up the Midland, Prudential, Lloyds, Mrs Ada Biggs and Mr Alan Platter. He gave it all to the poor, who blew it on Big Macs and chips.

Jack Straw asked him to join the Labour Party.

'Never, I'm an aristocrat!'

So Tony Blair made him Archer in Residence and he shot Labour members who got out of hand. He shot Mr Jack Straw. Ian Paisley fought back with bagpipes. Robin couldn't stand the noise so he shot the bagpipes. After this Robin was barred from Parliament and had to wait outside and shoot Labour candidates when they caused trouble or played bagpipes.

One day he saw Will Scarlet. He was a bus conductor.

'Robin, my old friend, stay on my bus all day for free.'

'Where is Big Dick?' asked Robin.

'He's a dustman in Hackney.'

'How terrible. He used to be my lieutenant. I'll find him.'

He did. He stood behind Big Dick's dustcart and got covered in it. Dick dug him out.

'Oh, my old leader, why don't we go and live in Sherwood. Unfortunately, Sherwood is only one tree nowadays.'

'Good, we'll hide behind it and wait for Midland Bank to go past and – wham bam!'

So they went back to Sherwood and hid behind a tree and, when Midland Bank went past, wham bam! But the bank told the police and they put Robin and Big Dick in the slammer.

'Do you want a solicitor?'

'Yes,' said Robin, 'I want Bing Crosby.'

Crosby's defence was: 'On behalf of my client I'd like to say:

Every time it rains it rains pennies from heaven
Don't you know each cloud contains pennies from heaven
You feel it falling all over town
That's why you hold your umbrella upside down
We need the showers
For sunshine and flowers
There'll be pennies from heaven
For you and me.

The Judge was a Bing Crosby fan. 'Case dismissed.'

Robin and Big Dick returned to the tree in Sherwood but they were unable to rob banks unless Bing Crosby said so. It started to rain so they both walked to the YMCA. They heard news of a great archery contest at Nottingham.

'That's for me,' said Robin, who was now 93.

The great day dawned. Twelve archers had entered. When it was Robin's turn, shaking like a leaf he fired his first arrow. It stuck in an oak tree. His second struck one of the spectators. Finally he hit the target plumb centre, and he was awarded the Golden Arrow With Jam Sandwich.

The Queen threw a great banquet. 'Robin Hood, my husband and my wifeless sons wish me to award you this bonnet and feather for you to become the Royal Archer.'

'Dear Queen, your husband and your wifeless sons, thank you. I would like permission to shoot a deer from the royal herd.'

'Of course. My husband and I and my wifeless sons grant you that wish.'

'Great Queen, ta.'

He climbed out of a window and shot one of the deer. The royal cook dressed it and served it to the company.

A coach and horses drove Robin and Marian back to their tree in Sherwood, where they settled down for the night in pouring rain.

'I think I'll die again. I'm getting fed up being alive.'

'Oh no, Robin, you're only 92.'

'But I'm bald.'

'That's why I've bought you this shoulder-length blond wig.'

'All right, I'll see how it goes and then I really must die. People are expecting it of me.'

Unfortunately, a great wind blew up and blew the wig hundreds of feet in the air and a man thought it was a pheasant and shot it. When Robin got it back it looked like a scarecrow and it had to be stuck down with UHU. He stuck it down on his forehead and couldn't see where he was going. Well, he wasn't going anywhere so it didn't matter.

'I'm not active enough,' said Robin.

'So shred this cabbage. Now peel the potatoes,' said Marian.

At potato no. 101 Robin collapsed. To revive him she threw a bucket of water over him and he recovered.

'No potato is going to beat me.'

On potato no. 102 he collapsed and had to be put to bed with a cup of Horlicks.

'I'll finish them tomorrow,' he said.

'Or they'll finish you.'

'Oh, we'll see, madame,' he said, sipping his Horlicks.

They saw, and the potatoes finished him.

'I'll do one a day,' he promised.

By potato no. 111 he was having giddy spells and had a fear of an elephant falling on him. To avoid it he slept in the clothes cupboard. Strangely enough an elephant fell on him. How it got in no one knows.

Because of his small body he applied to be a jockey. Lord Derby, the horse owner and gambler, took a liking to him and gave him a ride on Lion Heart at one hundred to one, an absolute outsider. It was the Gold Cup. At the start Lion Heart leapt from the gates. Robin clung on like a limpet under the horse. The horse went so fast he messed his pants. Lion Heart flew past the post; Robin hung on for dear life and fell off. Officials helped him up; the crowds cheered as he limped along. On the award stand Robin stroked Lion Heart; it bit him. Robin drew back and kicked him in the arse. The crowd booed, and a steward rushed Robin into the changing room where he changed into Gary Cooper in *The Bengal Lancers*.

'Mount,' said Cooper.

Robin mounted Lion Heart and 'Charge' came the order. Lion Heart, being a race horse, charged with Robin right through the enemy and out of sight on the other side. Lion Heart brought Robin back with him in his mouth.

'Absent on parade,' said Cooper. 'What's your excuse?'

'My horse is a race horse. He won the Gold Cup and he's just won it again!'

'Well, he won't win it any more,' said Cooper, and hung a hundred-pound anchor round his neck.

Robin told the RSPCA.

'You are fined one hundred rupees,' said the Magistrate.

'Time to pay,' said Cooper.

'Now is the time to pay, NOW!' said the Magistrate. 'What are you, a white American, doing in the Bengal Lancers?'

'You mean you knew all along I wasn't Indian?' Cooper broke into sobs; his shoulders shook; other bits not visible shook; he shook from head to foot.

Robin took him to England.

'Look,' said Marian, 'what *are* you doing out in India with Gary Cooper crying all over you? Look at you: you're soaking. You've been missing your medicines – a spoonful of Virol, one of Sanatogen, Halibut Liver Oil. Oh, your wig's on all wrong. Come back. They've built us a bungalow under our tree. The rain goes in but it gets out again.'

'I hate rain coming in.'

'Well, wait for it to go out again.'

'I'm in the Bengal Lancers; that's my horse with an anchor round its neck.'

'Why? He's not at sea,' said Maid Marian.

'He soon will be. They are going to throw him in it.'

'Won't that anchor drown him?'

'If he's not careful. Have you got a jam sandwich?'

'No, but I have deep-frozen porridge.'

'No, porridge makes me giddy and I keep falling down.'

'Well, try a small bite.'

He had a small bite, got giddy and kept falling down.

'He'll have to be hospitalised,' said a medic.

They put him on a stretcher but he kept falling off.

'Where's my three-legged dog called Rover who keeps falling over?'

They brought the ambulance.

'I'm not sick,' said Robin. 'I just keep falling. If I keep falling in that direction I can get to the hospital on my own.'

'Look, try falling upright: you'll get there quicker,' said Marian.

'Don't dare give me another porridge sandwich,' said Robin.

When they got to the hospital the Duchess of York was in the next bed.

'What are you doing here?' said Robin.

'I'm divorcing my husband; it's cheaper in an NHS hospital.'

Robin sat on the end of her bed.

'That's near enough,' she said, clutching her clothes, all made by Cheval of Paris.

'Would you have dinner with me?'

'Yes,' she said. 'Your bed or mine?'

'Neither,' said Robin. 'What's wrong with McDonald's?'

'Oh, if you eat there you get mad-cow's disease.'

'How do cows get mad-cow's disease?' said Robin.

'They eat at McDonald's,' said the Duchess.

'Let's have a Chinese takeaway,' said Robin. 'Hello, one portion of no. 3, one portion of no. 10, one portion of no. 20.'

They delivered but had added the numbers together and he had no. 33 – it was the washing-up water. 'It's delicious,' said Robin, going down with typhoid.

'Where's your husband?' said Robin.

'He's on a battleship,' said Fergie. 'He steers it.'

'Steers it where?' asked Robin.

'Away from the rocks. If he hits any the ship sinks.'

'What does he do?' said Robin.

'He throws everybody safely in the water then escapes in a helicopter.'

'Look, does he ever see the children?' Robin said.

'Yes, through a telescope.'

A telegram arrived for Robin.

'It's from the Queen,' said Robin. 'She wants me to go to the Palace, to give me the CBE and tea with Philip. You know Philip?' asked Robin.

'Do I?' said Fergie. 'He's my bloody father-in-law and landlord.'

'Oh I'll get him to reduce your rent, Fergie.'

Robin arrived in a horse and carriage with his bow.

'Hello, Robin,' said the Queen. 'This is Prince Philip.'

'Oh yes! He's Fergie's landlord.'

'What's that?' she said. 'What's that?' She pointed to his bow.

'It's for shooting.'

'Let's see you.'

So Robin shot a corgi.

'Oh, all over the carpet,' said the Queen. 'Corgis have been in my family for four hundred years.'

'Well, he was getting on. It's time he went. Shall I kill the rest?' said Robin.

'No. Now here's your CBE. Have your tea and leave,' said the Queen.

'Would you like a jam sandwich?' said Philip.

'Yes, I'll take it away with me,' said Robin, pointing to his mouth.

'Look,' said the Queen, holding a dead corgi bleeding down her dress, 'I want my CBE back. I'll put it with the Beatles' MBEs.'

'Come along, Robin. You can't be doing all this,' said Maid Marian. 'The Queen's bankrupt. She had to sell the royal yacht before it sank.'

'I've no merry men any more, only a merry woman, Maid Marian.'

Robin got a job as a floor manager. Sometimes he managed the ceiling; sometimes the floor, but the floor was his main job. He had to keep it clear of elephants. Unfortunately, a spare elephant got on it. He tried to shoo it but it fell on him and he was trapped underneath.

'Are you there, Robin? Don't worry, we'll call the fire brigade.'

Robin didn't understand. Was the elephant on fire? But when they arrived they pumped so much water on the elephant he drowned and they pulled Robin out. He was very flat and they had to inflate him. He floated up ten feet above the ground. A man from the fire brigade went up and brought him down by releasing the air through his toe.

'Where am I?' said Robin, regaining consciousness.

'England,' said Maid Marian, 'and you're very ill. You only weigh three ounces, as much as a Mars bar. Look at yourself.'

So he looked at himself and he wasn't there.

Robin ordered one hundred jam sandwiches, which

he ate till he weighed ten stone eleven pounds with jam oozing out of him.

'Look, you're going all over the carpet,' said Maid Marian. 'It's no good, the house is full of jam.'

'So am I,' said Robin.

Somehow the War Office had made a glaring mistake. Robin Hood was called up for the Navy.

'Can you swim?' said a recruiting sergeant.

'Why? Haven't you got any ships?' said Robin.

He was posted to a submarine.

'I'll stand on the pier and watch it go down,' said AB Robin Hood.

'You,' said the Admiral, 'you're supposed to be on that ship.'

'I'm excused from submarines due to claustrophobia. That sub had terrible claustrophobia. That's why half of the crew are clinging to the outside.'

'They're hiding!' roared the Admiral. 'They're all survivors from the last trip. Stand to attention!' said the Admiral.

Robin couldn't. He had piles.

'How long have you had them, man?' said the Admiral.

'Oh quite long. Sometimes they are two feet ten inches.'

'Come along, Robin,' said Maid Marian. 'I'm not having you serving in the Navy with piles. There's a bill for the corgi you shot. You can't go round shooting the Queen's corgis and get away with it.'

'I'll apologise to her.'

So he wrapped up a jam sandwich and added a note: 'Queen, I'm sorry I shot your corgi. Will you accept this jam sandwich with my best wishes?'

'Philip, come and taste this jam sandwich,' said the Queen. 'It's delicious. Send for Robin Hood at once!'

'If you like, Queen, I'll walk all your corgis in the park,' Robin offered.

So the Queen let him. Every one of them bit him on the leg; it went septic. In the hospital with his leg up the Queen came to say sorry.

'I'm very sorry.'

'You're sorry,' said Robin. 'You know, after they all bit me, each one pissed on my leg.'

'Oh, the dear little things.'

The next time he took them for a walk he kicked the shit out of them.

Philip took Robin for a pheasant shoot and before the day was out Robin had shot two gillies, a gun dog and wounded the Duke.

'Who said you could shoot?' raged the Duke.

'Albert J Scroff,' said Robin.

'Albert J Scroff? Who's he?' said the Duke.

'He's someone who said I could shoot,' said Robin.

'I'll sue him.'

Albert J Scroff was in the dock. 'Are you Albert J Scroff?'

'Only on Mondays; on Tuesdays I'm Goldie Hawn.'

'What day do you tell Robin Hood he can shoot?'

'That's the first Wednesday of the month.'

'You tell him he can shoot?'

'I've no idea if he can. I just say it. There's no law to stop me saying Robin Hood can shoot,' said Albert.

'Do you realise he shot two gillies, a gun dog and Prince Philip?'

'Oh I never said he could shoot gillies, gun dogs and Prince Philip. All I said was he can shoot and so he can. He shot two gillies, a gun dog and Prince Philip.'

The Judge banged his mallet.

'Silence in court. I want the accused to apologise to the gillies, the dog and Prince Philip. You will then be taken to a place and hanged.'

'I don't want to be hanged,' said Albert.

'They all say that,' said the Judge.

So Albert hung there until he'd hung long enough. They let him go. He was OK but his neck was a foot longer and he could see over people. On clear days he could see over the Channel, and saw the German Army waiting to invade England so he told Winston Churchill.

'Yes, I know,' said Churchill. 'I'm doing a painting of them before they do. Here, hold this rifle with five rounds. If they come, don't hesitate to shoot.'

Before he could shoot, they came.

Churchill was very angry. 'Get out of England at once or I'll tell Hitler. You've ruined my painting!'

He was so fierce they all got out of England. So he told Hitler. 'Listen, Adolph.'

'*Ya*, I am listening.'

'Your German Army ruined my painting.'

'Ach, as a painter myself I understand your feeling.'

Hitler then had twenty soldiers shot to set an example.

'Winston, what do I do with this rifle and five rounds?' said Robin.

'You can guard the people of England against an overdraft.'

So Robin shot thirteen bank managers.

'Come on, Robin, you can't shoot bank managers and get away with it.'

But he did. Thirteen bank managers he had notched up on the butt of his gun. If he went in a bar they all dived for cover. 'He's the Bank Manager Killer!' they gasped.

Robin was fifty for the second time but still had a good figure, £50,000 to be precise. He opened a sandwich bar, boasting that he could make any sandwich a customer desired.

'Can I have an elephant sandwich?' said a customer.

'How many?' said Robin.

'One,' said the customer.

'Bugger off, I'm not going to kill an elephant for one sandwich,' said Robin.

Robin wanted to be a skater in *Starlight Express* but on skates at the audition he raced round the track and shot off it straight out the stage door and collided with a lamppost and broke both ankles. Thank heaven he was a member of BUPA and had a luxurious room with a po under the bed. Lloyd Webber came to commiserate and gave Robin a bottle of champagne. Robin sprayed it all over Webber, who sued him.

*

'Did you, without malice aforethought, spray Lord Webber with champagne?' said the Judge.

'Yes, m'lud,' said Robin. 'Racing-car drivers do it.'

'Lord Webber isn't a racing-car driver,' said the Judge.

'How was I to know that?' said Robin.

'Do you agree, Lord Webber, that you don't look like a racing-car driver?' said the Judge.

'No, I look like a composer of successful musicals,' said Webber.

'How does the jury find?' said the Judge.

'We find that Lord Webber looks like a composer of successful musicals.'

'How do you find Robin Hood?' said the Judge.

'We find him an old man in bed with fractured ankles.'

'What about damages?' said Webber.

'He's got enough damages, both ankles,' said the Judge. 'Case dismissed.'

'We have to X-ray your wallet, Mr Hood,' said a doctor. 'Don't worry, it won't hurt. We just want to know if you can afford to be in BUPA.'

So Robin changed the locks on his wallet. They X-rayed the wallet – he was skint, so they wheeled him out of the hospital and put him on a 137 bus which wasn't going anywhere. Robin didn't want to go anywhere – so he stayed on till it got there. He got off and sure enough he wasn't anywhere. Brixton is anywhere so he went there.

'Hello there,' said a tall black man. 'Welcome to Brixton.'

'You're welcome to it, too.'

'Don't be like that.'

'I've always been like this. What have you been like?'

'I've been like Frank Bruno,' said the man, and knocked Robin down. 'What a pity you aren't Mike Tyson.'

So for a moment Robin became Mike Tyson and knocked Frank Bruno down.

'That will be one million dollars,' said Robin. 'I think I'll retire from the ring now.' And Robin bought a Rolls Royce, and drove to Maid Marian under the tree in Sherwood Forest.

'What have you got there?' said Maid Marian, giving herself a flu jab.

'It's my new home,' said Robin, beeping the horn.

'You come on here and have your flu jab and tea.'

'What's for tea?' said Robin.

'A flu jab and a boiled egg,' said Marian.

'Could you give my flu jab to the boiled egg?' said Robin.

'Silly, boiled eggs don't catch flu,' said Marian.

'Not if they're given a flu jab,' said Robin.

Robin drove Maid Marian to the South of France in the Rolls Royce. It took him a while to find it. He missed it three times.

Finding himself alone in Rome he realised he was lost again – but by eating twelve plates of spaghetti at gun point, he escaped from Italy. Pursued by twelve Fascists and a beautiful Italian ballerina, he shook off the Fascists and she shook him off.

'Leave Marian,' she said.

'No, she does my laundry,' he said.

'I'll do your laundry in champagne with you in it,' said the beautiful ballerina.

So she did it in champagne and him in it. She hung him up to dry, pissed. She left him there all night till he was sober.

'Looka, I introduce-a you-a to Mussolini,' she said.

'Benito, dis is the famous bandit Robin Hood.'

'Oh gooda, have some spaghetti.'

'No thanks, I've just eaten twelve plates at pistol point.'

'OK, then have some ice cream.'

So Robin had an ice cream while Mussolini pointed a pistol.

'What's that for?' said Robin.

'It's in case you don't eat your ice cream. All British POWs we catch eat ice cream at pistol point.'

'What if they won't eat it?' said Robin.

'We-ar paint them green with yellow spots.'

'Does that contravene the Geneva Convention?' said Robin.

'No, no, no. Where does it say you mustn't paint your enemy?' said Mussolini.

'I'm not going to eat this ice cream,' said Robin.

Mussolini painted him green with yellow spots.

'Does this mean I'm a prisoner of war?' said Robin.

'*Si si,*' said Mussolini, and drove him to a POW camp.

Robin's first words were: 'Helppp. I want out! I've never declared war on anyone except the pigeons in Trafalgar Square!'

'*Silencio*! You'll give us all away,' said the camp commander.

'I want to escape,' said Robin.

So they let him out the back. Splash! He was in Venice.

'Get me out before I get typhoid!'

And he got typhoid. In hospital his temperature soared so they hooked him up to the central heating and that winter he kept the whole hospital warm. He nearly died from typhoid but he decided against it and settled for an itch. He started scratching it in April and didn't stop till Christmas but by then he had nearly scratched himself away.

Maid Marian collected him in the Rolls pulled by a donkey.

'It's run out of petrol. Who's that woman in your bed?' she said, sticking a knife in her.

'She's a grievously wounded Italian,' said Robin. 'She did my washing in champagne. She was a one-off.'

'Well, she's really off now,' said Marian, tipping her down the rubbish chute.

'Have you been sleeping with her?' said Marian.

'No,' said Robin, 'I've been sleeping with Mussolini.'

'Why are you green with yellow spots?' said Marian.

'You get that from sleeping with Mussolini.'

Then Robin died of green with yellow spots. It had been a good life.

Maid Marian married Jimmy Saville, thus putting an end to his career.

BLACK BEAUTY
According to Spike Milligan

Next was to break me harness. First, a stiff heavy collar on my neck. Then there was a bridle with great side-pieces called blinkers against my eyes. Then there was a small saddle strap that went under my tail; that was the crapper. I hated it, it stopped me having a crap. I never felt more like kicking so I kicked him in the goolies and they swelled up like water melons. He had to put the harness on me while balancing his balls with one hand and could only move very slowly. In time I got used to everything (and he got used to swollen balls) and I could do my work as well as my mother. I used to wash up after dinner. Yes, I was a very good horse.

ISBN 0-7535-0102-3
£5.99 pb

FRANKENSTEIN
According to Spike Milligan

How can I describe my emotions at this catastrophe, or delineate the wretch whom with such infinite pains and care I had endeavoured to form? There was the bolt that affixed his neck to his spine, there were the screws holding his forehead to his skull; but now was the moment of truth. I plunged the electrodes into his rectum and switched on the current. He gave a groan and he was alive. He spoke as he sat up, 'Have you got a fag mate?' My God, I had given birth to a nicotine junky! I handed him a cigarette which I lit, then, leaping off the table, he stood there. But, alas, we had forgotten one thing. He had no support for his trousers which fell to the floor revealing his manhood in all its glory. If any women saw it they would be leaving their husbands in thousands. Quickly I got some string round his trousers. What had I done? No mortal could support the horror of that countenance! I rushed downstairs, to seek refuge in a cupboard where I remained during the rest of the night walking up and down in great agitation, something difficult to do in a cupboard.

ISBN 0-7535-0227-5
£5.99 pb

THE GOONS
THE STORY
ed. Norma Farnes

The Goons first came together in a pub called The Grafton Arms in London's Victoria. The pub was a popular meeting place for actors, comics and writers in the early post-war years, with landlord and scriptwriter Jimmy Grafton serving up advice and encouragement along with the beer. Spike Milligan was renting a room above the pub and working on comedy scripts with Grafton – who became known as KOGVOS, King of the Goons and Voice of Sanity – when his wartime friend Harry Secombe introduced him to Peter Sellers and Michael Bentine.

There then began a terrible rasping, squealing, giggling, snorting period of lunacy which continued unabated until 1960. The Goons first went on air at the BBC as *The Crazy People* on 28 May 1951. It wasn't until the second series in January 1952 that the BBC agreed to their changing the name of the show to *The Goon Show*. Spike Milligan, of course, became the driving force behind the Goons, writing the scripts and devising the characters which became part of our comedy heritage.

There is still a huge interest in the Goons, with each new generation discovering afresh the anarchic humour which has had such a massive influence on so many of our top comedy performers.

This unique collection of Spike's personal memorabilia and photographs, along with contributions from Sir Harry Secombe (the only other surviving Goon and co-writer of two dozen Goon shows), Eric Sykes, and a select band of Goons aficionados, forms a fascinating history of this enduring comic phenomenon.

ISBN 0-7535-0529-0
£9.99 pb

THE HOUND OF THE BASKERVILLES
According to Spike Milligan

Published to coincide with Spike's 80th Birthday celebrations, this strictly limited edition is a lavishly produced volume in an antique style with gold blocking on the front and spine, covered with a leather cloth and featuring a padded front board. The high specification makes this a very desirable addition to any Milligan fan's collection and it is the jewel in the crown of Virgin's 80th Birthday Promotion for Spike.

Spike's hilarious version of Conan Doyle's classic mystery is quite unique. Sherlock Holmes needs all of his famous skills of logic and deduction along with Dr Watson's loyal assistance to investigate the strange affair of *The Hound of The Baskervilles*. At the request of the eminent Dr James Mortimer, Holmes and Watson set out to unravel the mysterious events at Baskerville Hall, including the sinister death of Sir Charles Baskerville and the curious occurrences on the desolate moor. In the black of night, the moor plays host to any number of foul deeds with lovers enjoying secret trysts, butterfly collectors on the rampage, escaped convicts evading capture and a howling hound called Eric terrorising the neighbourhood.

Dr Watson wouldn't know what to make of it. Sherlock Holmes would surely heave a great sigh and light up one of his 'special' pipes.

ISBN 0-7535-0670-X
£5.99 pb

A MAD MEDLEY OF MILLIGAN
Spike Milligan

Said Prince Charles
When they placed
The Crown on his head
I suppose this means
That Mummy's dead

A new collection of Spike's poems, jokes, doodles, giggles and general hilarity – including the historical epic 'Adolf Hitler, Dictator and Clown'.

ISBN 0-7535-0779-X
£4.99 pb

A CHILDREN'S TREASURY OF MILLIGAN
Classic Stories & Poems by
Spike Milligan

This unique anthology of Spike's poems and stories for children presents his classic children's books in a way they have never been seen before. The large, hardback format gives ample scope to make the most of Spike's own illustrations, lovingly coloured specially for this book.

The anthology comprises *Silly Verse for Kids* (1959), *The Bald Twit Lion* (1968), *A Book of Milliganimals* (1968), *Unspun Socks from a Children's Laundry* (1981), *Sir Nobonk and the Terrible, Awful, Dreadful, Naughty, Nasty Dragon* (1982) and *Startling Verse For All The Family* (1987).

Spike does not regard children as small grown-ups, but as an entirely different species who live in a secret, magical world, which very few adults understand. His poems were inspired by listening to his own children, and subsequently his grandchildren, and marvelling at the way they could invent new words or incorporate sound effects into their everyday language.

In 'borrowing' their language, Spike has created a range of poems and stories which are a delight to read to younger children, for older children to read themselves, or for grown-ups to recapture some of the magic.

ISBN 0-7535-0454-5
£9.99 pb

SPIKE MILLIGAN THE FAMILY ALBUM: AN ILLUSTRATED AUTOBIOGRAPHY

For years Spike Milligan has lovingly collected and collated over a dozen precious volumes of family photographs and memorabilia, stretching from Army life in India in 1869, his birth in 1918 and his childhood, to his life as an entertainer, and the arrival of his own family. Spike has carefully selected scores of these very personal photographs to illustrate his intriguing family history and the story of his career, creating a fascinating record of his amazing life.

In writing *The Family Album* Spike has overcome a major personal hurdle. At times touching and deeply intimate, this book includes details of how Spike was plagued by manic depression; stemming from his wartime experiences, his traumatic mental breakdown, and the collapse of his first marriage, all of which has led him to believe that he could never write an autobiography such as this. *The Family Album* is an inspiring, poignant retrospective from a true comic genius.

ISBN 1-85227-886-2
£20.00 hb